Advance praise fc
The Looting of Ame

"Les Leopold's book is a cogent, clear, and compelling explanation of how Wall Street's Big Casino wrecked the economy. I might not agree with all of his provocative proposals, but so what? This book is a fun read, despite the sickening scenario it describes."

—JONATHAN ALTER, Senior Editor and Columnist at *Newsweek* and author of the bestselling book *The Defining Moment: FDR's Hundred Days and the Triumph of Hope*

"Les Leopold has given an entertaining account of the growth of the derivative market that supported the housing bubble during the last decade and offers useful recommendations for avoiding the next bubble-and-bust. He is one of the few observers to have understood how today's crisis has roots going back three decades and to have seen how it connects to the upward redistribution of income over this period."

—DEAN BAKER, co-director of the Center for Economic and Policy Research and author of *Plunder and Blunder: The Rise and Fall of the Bubble Economy*

"Les Leopold's account of the economic crisis is the clearest and most accessible that I have seen. It gives a reader with little economics or financial background a riveting description of how Wall Street tore down our economy and what we can do about it. It's a page turner we all should read."

—LEO GERARD, International President of the United Steelworkers

"Les Leopold tells the story of our economic collapse so clearly, so broadly, so stylishly I didn't get lost; in fact, to my great surprise, I kept going and going like Hansel and Gretel through the thick forest of mortgage finance, credit swaps, bubbles, and bailouts. *The Looting of America* is a guided tour for people who wonder if the ups and downs of a free market are inevitable, or if we can't make a few changes for a smoother ride."

—ROBERT KRULWICH, NPR Science Correspondent and co-host of *Radio Lab*

THE LOOTING OF AMERICA

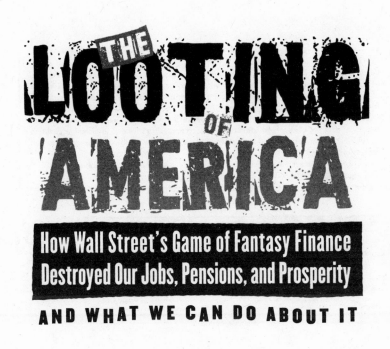

THE LOOTING OF AMERICA

How Wall Street's Game of Fantasy Finance Destroyed Our Jobs, Pensions, and Prosperity

AND WHAT WE CAN DO ABOUT IT

LES LEOPOLD

CHELSEA GREEN PUBLISHING

WHITE RIVER JUNCTION, VERMONT

Project Manager: Emily Foote
Developmental Editor: Jonathan Teller-Elsberg
Copy Editor: Cannon Labrie
Proofreader: Helen Walden
Indexer: Lee Lawton
Designer: Peter Holm, Sterling Hill Productions

Printed in Canada
First printing April 2009
10 9 8 7 6 5 4 3 2 1   09 10 11 12 13

Our Commitment to Green Publishing
Chelsea Green sees publishing as a tool for cultural change and ecological stewardship. We strive
to align our book manufacturing practices with our editorial mission and to reduce the impact
of our business enterprise on the environment. We print our books and catalogs on chlorine-
free recycled paper, using vegetable-based inks whenever possible. This book may cost slightly
more because we use recycled paper, and we hope you'll agree that it's worth it. Chelsea Green
is a member of the Green Press Initiative (www.greenpressinitiative.org), a nonprofit coalition
of publishers, manufacturers, and authors working to protect the world's endangered forests and
conserve natural resources.

The Looting of America was printed on Legacy TB Natural, a 100-percent postconsumer recycled paper supplied by Webcom.

Preserving our environment
Chelsea Green Publishing Co. chose to print the pages of this
book on recycled paper and saved these resources[1]:

ANCIENT FOREST™ FRIENDLY

109 trees were saved for our forests

energy	water	greenhouse gases	solid waste
76 million BTUs	39,901 gal.	9,613 lbs	5,124 lbs

Printed by **Webcom Inc.**
on Legacy TB Natural 100% post-consumer waste.

FSC
Mixed Sources
Product group from well-managed
forests, controlled sources and
recycled wood or fiber
Cert no. SW-COC-002358
www.fsc.org
© 1996 Forest Stewardship Council

[1]Estimates were made using the Environmental Defense Paper Calculator.

Library of Congress Cataloging-in-Publication Data
Leopold, Les.
   The looting of America : how Wall Street's game of fantasy finance destroyed our jobs, pensions, and
prosperity, and what we can do about it / Les Leopold.
      p. cm.
   Includes index.
   ISBN 978-1-60358-205-6
   1. Finance--United States. 2. Financial crises--United States. 3. United States--Economic condi-
tions--2001- 4. United States--Economic policy--2001- I. Title.

   HG181.L42 2009
   330.973--dc22

                                 2009014181

Chelsea Green Publishing Company
Post Office Box 428
White River Junction, VT 05001
(802) 295-6300
www.chelseagreen.com

Contents

Acknowledgments

For me, it takes a village to raise a book. The staff of the Labor Institute, with whom I have had the privilege to work for the past several decades, provided incredible support. I'm deeply indebted to Joe Anderson, Kathy Burris, Paul Renner, Sally Silvers, Rodrigo Toscano, Jean Urano, and Jim Young for the time, space, encouragement, and insight they provided. Thanks also to Mark Dudzic, Maureen Keegan, and Michael Merrill for their careful comments on the draft.

Also special thanks to Jim Frederick and Mike Gill of the United Steelworkers, who have consistently encouraged me to innovate and write. Joe Kiriaki, the executive director of the Kenosha Teachers Association, also provided invaluable help guiding me through the financial doings of Wisconsin, and proving again how hard good union reps work for justice each day. And my thanks to David Schlein of the National Educational Association, who encouraged me to spread this information to teachers all across the country.

Much encouragement also came from my merry band of cousins (and second cousins and cousins-in-law) who took the time to read drafts and egg me on. Many thanks to Jeff, Sandy, Chuck, Diane, and Alejandro. And a special thanks to Norman and Debbie for their comments and support, and for hosting so many events that have kept our extended family together. My sister Evelyn also inspired this work—as a professional journalist, she has set a very high bar for integrity and accuracy toward which the rest of us can only aspire.

I was lucky again to have the invaluable editorial help of Laura McClure. Her combination of skill, politics, good cheer, and encouragement is impossible to beat. You need a freelance editor? Get her! I was also very fortunate again to enlist David Dembo to provide research and editorial support. His deep commitment to social justice shines through all his efforts and helps light the way for books like this.

The Chelsea Green Publishing staff is a joy to work with, starting with the publisher, Margo Baldwin, and editorial director, Joni Praded. When they decide to back a book, they go for it with gusto. A special thanks to Jonathan Teller-Elsberg, who enthusiastically edited the final draft with me. His insight, meticulous fact checking, and economic expertise have made this a much better book.

Bill Lee, my agent, again put in much more time than he should have. Maybe someday he'll get paid back for all the help he has provided. All I can offer now is my deepest appreciation for his friendship and expertise. Jim Young, another good friend, colleague, and neighbor also helped guide this book to its home. I owe him plenty.

I'm also deeply indebted to the financial soccer dads in our town who took the time to educate this money-and-banking ignoramus. They, too, care about this crisis and want to build a better world for our kids.

And finally comes the heart of my village—Dr. Sharon Szymanski, my lifelong partner. As the one true economist of the family, she provided a never-ending stream of articles, information, and insight. But most importantly, her love makes all of this happen. We're blessed with two great kids, Chester and Lilah, who provide more encouragement than they ever will realize. They are so much of the reason Sharon and I strive to build a better world.

Introduction

Okay, you got this far, which means you already know something important: that you don't know enough about the financial toxic waste Wall Street has foisted upon us. Sure, you've heard there are piles of bad mortgages taken out by people who couldn't afford them. You've also heard that all of us, consumers and bankers alike, are too deeply in debt and that it's time to tighten our belts. But you suspect that's not really the entire story. It isn't.

Like most of us, you are praying that the stimulus package and the Wall Street bailouts will resurrect the economy (although you're probably dubious about helping wealthy bankers, and furious with their bloated bonuses). You're also worried that as the economy crashes your hopes and dreams for our country—like universal health care or alternative energy investments or renewed support for public education—are slipping out of reach. And you no doubt fear the country will be crushed under the mountain of debt that we are accumulating. It's all a muddle, and you'd like some straight answers. Same here.

After the housing bubble burst in 2007, I realized I didn't know enough about modern high finance. The last economics textbook I cracked open devoted 544 pages to the production of goods and services, and only one page to banking and finance. It couldn't explain why our economy was collapsing and why we had to give all that money to Wall Street to avoid an even worse collapse. I no longer felt like an informed citizen. It was time to figure some of it out and share it with my fellow ignoramuses.

I turned to the experts, the way we're supposed to. I studied the analyses of the bankers, investment analysts, scholars, and reporters who are trying to explain this mess or propose solutions to it. But too many experts are wearing ideological blinders. Many of these insiders formed the cheerleading chorus when all was rosy and billions were being made on Wall Street. Almost all promoted our bright new financial-services economy as the way forward for America. And they considered anyone who questioned it to be an inconsequential whiner or a radical kook. What's more, most insiders seemed unable even to ask whether the new wave of "financial engineering" contributed to or harmed our society. Instead, their understanding was: "If it makes that much money, it *must* be good, useful, and productive."

It's very hard from the inside to question market fundamentalism. We have been told for decades that private-sector financial markets are, by definition, the most efficient way to allocate capital. And if they aren't working efficiently, it must mean government has interfered and messed them up. This faith-based thinking has pervaded all of our established institutions and financial reporting. It's even taught in our grade schools.

In this book, I come at the economic crisis from outside the usual professions. I aim to answer some very basic questions and share what I've learned in a way that will allow others to understand it too. As we investigate the nitty-gritty of the crisis, we'll also make sure to keep a big-picture perspective. This crisis is a good thirty years in the making, and we won't solve anything if "solutions" don't address the underlying issues.

To maintain our citizenship in a world dominated by imploding economies, we all need some basic financial literacy. I mean, take a look around you: We are teetering on the edge of a vast economic depression. The experts helped us get here. You want to let them write all the critiques as well?

———

For the past few years, I've had a morbid curiosity about exotic financial instruments, especially collateralized debt obligations (CDOs)—those highly profitable new financial products that supposedly made housing more affordable to marginal buyers and generated vast sums for the financial sector at almost no risk for investors. (To keep the terms straight, there's a glossary in back. I'll also be explaining the guts of CDOs in chapter 6.) Wall Streeters and their cheerleaders in the media told us that these

CDOs were part of a wave of great new products from American financial institutions that were making our country strong and rich. As we ceased to be a manufacturing giant, we were becoming the great engine of global financial innovation, spewing forth these wondrous new inventions. In fact, these new financial instruments, the envy of the world, were said to be much more profitable than making cars or steel or refrigerators. And they produced high-paying jobs, which in turn helped increase our overall standard of living—especially in Manhattan!

It was really hard to understand how these instruments worked. I kept imagining something like a financial iPod—an elegant new device that gave people something they really wanted (or thought they had to have), and in return earned profits galore for those who produced it. But as I read more about my imaginary CDO-iPod, I soon realized that there was something fundamentally different about a financial product and a consumer product: namely, when a financial product screws up, the entire world economy could collapse.

As of this writing, several trillion dollars' worth of value—something close to half of all the world's financial wealth—has disappeared from the global economy due to, or facilitated in large part by, fundamentally flawed CDO products.[1] Our government is bailing out Wall Street firms and has taken over Fannie Mae and Freddie Mac, two companies at the heart of our mortgage system. Lehman Brothers has gone into liquidation, Merrill Lynch's bull has been gored by the Bank of America, and now Bank of America is in serious trouble. Along the way, the largest insurance company in the world, AIG, is essentially owned by the taxpayer, and Citigroup is not far behind. Meanwhile, banks are doing precious little lending, and the economic system is spiraling down with unemployment rising rapidly well into 2009. And the government has been forced to spend nearly $1 trillion on financial bailouts and another $787 billion on a public stimulus package to keep the economy from tumbling into the abyss.

These innovative financial products also are polluting local treasuries around the globe. The town of Narvik, located at the northern tip of Norway, invested its reserve funds in supposedly supersafe CDOs: It lost $65 million. Five Wisconsin school districts invested $35 million and borrowed $165 million more to purchase AA-rated securities called "synthetic" CDOs. Not only are they now on the verge of losing their entire investment, but they also owe $200 million. That's some financial product!

As with other defective products, there's a recall underway—the largest product recall in history. These financial instruments, which sliced and diced mortgages into securities sold and resold all over the world, have grown so toxic that they have to be carefully removed from the balance sheets of banks, investment houses, brokerages, insurance firms, and other financial entities. (I can't help picturing bank examiners fully encapsulated in white hazmat suits and air packs, using large tweezers to pluck the toxic products from the banks' books.) In fact, these financial hazards are turning out to be so toxic that the Bush administration, in November 2008, gave up trying to remove them and instead partially nationalized key portions of the banking system, while also providing tens of billions to other key financial institutions. Imagine that—a product so toxic that the virulently free-market Bush White House adopted socialist policies!

But this product recall is like no other. Rather than being reeled back in by their corporate producers owing to their faulty design, the federal government at first decided to use at least 700 billion of our tax dollars to buy the products from the ailing banks. (Some say we're already up to $1.5 trillion when you count federal guarantees, and the total will go even higher before it's over.) Then they decided that instead of buying up the toxic waste, they would loan billions of dollars to the polluted financial companies to get them, in turn, to lend money to businesses and consumers again. (Meanwhile, the Federal Reserve was quietly insuring the toxic assets, which may cost us hundreds of billions of dollars more down the road.) Now the Obama administration is again taking up the plan to remove these hazardous assets from the banks, which could end up requiring several *trillion* dollars on top of the money already put into this mess. Meanwhile, Wall Street's finest awarded themselves $18.4 billion in bonuses for a job well done during the worst financial crash since the Great Depression, *after* their banks went on the federal dole.

Compare this to the failure of a more tangible product like an iPod. Let's imagine that a major electrical problem was discovered that caused iPods to burst into flames (the way some laptop-computer batteries made by Sony actually have done[2]). If the cost of the recall and the threat of legal action were enough to totally sink Apple, Inc.—which is pretty unlikely—about $90 billion (as of this writing) would evaporate as the company's stock crashed to zero. That's spare change compared to a CDO going haywire. As we are learning day by day, the demise of faulty financial products can ignite a vast economic firestorm.

Another tremendous difference between a CDO financial instrument and an iPod is that, as of this writing, no one on earth really knows how much a given CDO is worth. As a result, banks, investment houses, and insurance companies—which are loaded with these products—are struggling to figure out whether or not they are solvent. And since they know that they don't know, they also know that *others* don't know. They don't trust each other, and investors don't trust them. Unlike the iPod, with its "suggested retail" sticker price, the value of many CDOs often can be estimated only through complex computer models. And no one trusts the models either. Hence a great freeze in the credit and loans our system relies upon.

How could this alleged pillar of our nation's grand financial future be so "opaque"? How is it possible that this shady instrument might damage the entire world economy? And how come so few of us have any idea how it works? Writers and policy makers are talking a good game about how people took loans they couldn't afford, and how these were put in mortgage securities that have crashed in value, and that these mysterious CDOs somehow have caused the housing market to tank (or is it the other way around?). You hear them use the word *tranche* (the French word for "slice") with intimate familiarity as if it were a new type of croissant. But if you listen carefully, you can sense that they have only the vaguest understanding of how these new financial instruments work . . . and don't work.

And how many policy makers and analysts are willing to step back and look at what we've really become? Our nation has entrusted trillions of dollars of investment and debt to the creators and distributors of these indecipherable instruments. We've written rules, or eliminated rules, or failed to write rules that have encouraged the creation of wildly complex and (at one time) wildly profitable financial arrangements that turned out to be lethal. We've allowed a new global shadow banking system to exist totally beyond the control of any regulatory body. We've given the swashbuckling, gambling, high-risk alpha males and females of finance the keys to our economy and they've crashed it.

We have put our collective livelihoods at risk, and for what? Why have tens of thousands of our very best minds spent their energies dreaming up new money-making-money instruments that may be at best socially neutral and at worst disastrous? At this perilous moment for our planet, why are so many talented people spending their days playing this extremely risky game of fantasy finance?

I've tried to keep an open mind about the social utility of CDOs and other newfangled financial instruments—and the tens of thousands of truly bright people who make, sell, and profit by them. But the evidence just keeps mounting that much of the financial sector, as currently constructed, is basically a drain on our resources. Commentators everywhere point to the unproductive deployment of talent in financial engineering when we really need more minds engineering clean energy alternatives, among other things. They also are quick to slam Wall Street for its greed as if this were a freshly observed quality. Since when has greed been a sin on Wall Street or in capitalism as a whole? In fact, it's supposed to be the very best motivator for creating efficiency in a market economy. Didn't Adam Smith long ago suggest that by narrowly pursuing our individual interests, society prospers?

And prosper it did. The financial sector, up until the 2008 crash, was one of the fastest growing sectors of the economy, generating approximately 20 percent of our gross domestic product. It also accounted for 27.4 percent of all corporate profits.[3] Finance grew as manufacturing declined, thereby dominating the real economy. According to the Bureau of Labor Statistics, in 1940 there were 7.1 manufacturing jobs for every job in the financial service industries. The ratio increased to 7.7 in 1950. Then the slide started, as you can see in chart 1. By November 2008, *there were only 1.6 manufacturing jobs per financial services job.* Until the current meltdown, the financial industry produced almost 10 percent of all the wages and salaries in the country, up from 5 percent in 1975. In a few years, provided that the system doesn't collapse entirely, the finance sector is going to be larger than the manufacturing economy.

When we hear that these financial institutions are too big to fail, unfortunately it's because they are. As of 2008, Citigroup, Bank of America, JPMorgan Chase, and AIG had revenues of

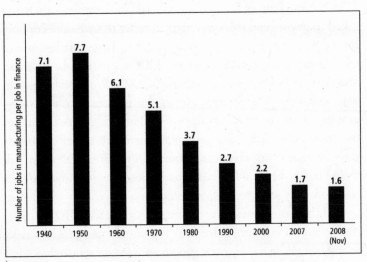

Chart 1. U.S. Job Ratio: Manufacturing to Finance Bureau of Labor Statistics

over $100 billion each. Goldman Sachs and Morgan Stanley were not far behind, each with approximately $80 billion in revenues.[4] If all of them were to fail simultaneously, then all of us, as distant as we might think we are from the day-to-day operations of Wall Street, would be staring at another Great Depression.

I'm worried that Wall Street wizards have used exotic financial instruments to set up a vast game of fantasy finance . . . betting with other people's money. Is it possible that a handful of bankers and traders are making huge sums of very real money by creating, buying, and selling financial products that add little to the real economy? Is this like fantasy baseball leagues where prizes are won based on stats derived from the real game of baseball?

There are at least a couple of very obvious differences: In fantasy baseball, a few dollars exchange hands at the end of the season and no one would dare claim that make-believe baseball improves real Major League Baseball. In fantasy finance, trillions of dollars change hands and, until recently, our financial leaders—Alan Greenspan, Robert Rubin, and the like—claimed that the game actually helped to improve the real-world economy. Unfortunately for us, they were mistaken.

To be sure, fantasy finance is very real. We taxpayers are being asked to pay several trillion dollars in order to save our economy from collapse by bailing out Wall Street in large part because of their latest and greatest products—CDOs, credit default swaps, and their unholy spawn, "synthetic" CDOs. We are also paying with our jobs. The jobless rate in the private sector is rising rapidly, climbing to 8.5 percent by March 2009. And public-sector workers, from teachers to firemen, are under assault as state and local tax revenues plummet. I'm sure all of us at risk would like to know a bit more about these financial instruments and how they are wrecking our economy.

And then there's the subprime-mortgage puzzle. The financial media has all but concluded that the crash was caused by risky mortgages taken out by poor people and deadbeats who couldn't afford them, and issued by reckless lenders who should have known better. About $1.3 trillion worth of such mortgages are out there. Of that, about $300 billion are in default or nearly so (divided equally between the subprime and Alt-A mortgages, the two riskiest types). Please, can someone explain how that amount, about 2 percent of household net worth, could devastate the world's financial system? To date, the taxpayer has put up about $2 trillion in bank bailouts and loan guarantees. Why didn't that take care of the problem long ago? Like some perverse modern-day miracle of fishes and loaves, how did $300 billion of bad debt multiply into trillions of dollars in financial toxic waste? Poor people did all that?

In this book I go after these questions—and I hope the answers will tell us a good deal about our economic woes and what to do about them. At the very least, I hope to contribute modestly to our collective financial literacy.

In short, if I can understand this crap, so can you.

one

The Hooking of Whitefish Bay

THE GREAT ECONOMIC CRASH of 2008 tore right through Whitefish Bay, Wisconsin, population 13,500—though you'd never guess it from looking around town.

Located just a few miles north of Milwaukee, this golden village exudes the hopeful self-confidence of the early 1960s. Whitefish Bay's stately mansions offer breathtaking views of Lake Michigan from cliffs that rise a hundred feet above the shoreline. As you head inland on its tree-lined streets, the houses slowly shrink back into sturdy, middle-class neighborhoods. The stores on Silver Spring Drive, its main shopping strip, have survived despite fierce competition from the nearby Bayshore Mall (a self-contained ultramodern shopping village with faux streets, a faux town square, and real condos). Whitefish Bay also supports an art deco movie theater that serves meals while you watch the show, and a top-notch supermarket, fish market, and bakery. Nothing is out of place—except you, if you happen to be brown or black. Whitefish Bay is 94 percent white and only 1 percent black. There's a reason the town's unfortunate moniker is White Folks Bay.

Yet this white-collar town voted for Obama—and has always voted for its schools, which are considered among the best in the state. Its residents' deep pockets supply the school system with all the extras: In 2007, $700,000 in donations provided "opportunities, services and facilities for students." The investment has paid off. An average of 94 percent of Whitefish Bay's high school graduates go on to college immediately. And the school dropout rate is less than half of 1 percent.

The school district takes its fiscal responsibilities seriously. It has set up a trust fund to pay benefits, primarily health insurance, for retired school employees. When these benefits (called "Other Post-Employment Benefits" or OPEB) were originally negotiated, the expense was modest. But then health care costs exploded. What's more, accounting rules now require that school districts amortize these costs and post them on their books as a liability each year. Whitefish Bay, like many other school districts, became worried about how to meet these liabilities.

Whitefish Bay is a town full of financially sophisticated residents, including its school managers. They sought to pump up the OPEB trust fund quickly so they could keep their promises to retirees. As responsible guardians of the town's resources, they looked for the highest rate of return at a minimal risk to the fund's principal. As Shaun Yde, the school district's director of business services, put it, the goal was to "guarantee a secure future for our employees without increasing the burden on our taxpayers or decreasing the funds available to our students to fund their education."[1]

Meanwhile, Wall Street investment houses had set their sights on school-district trust funds like Whitefish Bay's. They hoped to persuade districts to stop stashing this money—valued at well above $100 billion nationwide in 2006—in treasury bonds and federally insured certificates of deposit (CDs). Wall Street's "innovative" securities could provide higher returns—not to mention more lucrative fees for the investment firms.

So an old-fashioned financial romance began: Supply (Wall Street's hottest financial products) met Demand (school districts seeking to build up their OPEB trust funds). It looked like a perfect match.

In the Milwaukee area, Supply was represented by Stifel Nicolaus & Company, a venerable, 108-year-old financial firm, which promised to put "the welfare of clients and community first" as it pursued "excellence and a desire to exceed clients' expectations . . ."[2]

As a national firm based in St. Louis, Stifel Nicolaus was fortunate to be represented in Milwaukee by David W. Noack. According to the *New York Times*, "He had been advising Wisconsin school boards for two decades, helping them borrow for new gymnasiums and classrooms. His father had taught at an area high school for 47 years. All six of his children attended Milwaukee schools."[3] School boards repeatedly referred to him as their "financial advisor"—a label he never refuted.[4]

In 2006, Mr. Noack, an avuncular, low-key salesman (he preferred to be called a banker), urged the Whitefish school board and others in Wisconsin to buy securities that offered higher returns than treasury notes but were just about as safe. He had recently attended a two-hour training session on these new financial products, so he was confident when he assured the officials that they were "safe double-A, triple-A-type investments." None of the investments included subprime debt, he said. And the deal conformed to state statutes, so the district would be erring on the conservative side. In fact, Noack said, the risk was so low that there would have to be "15 Enrons" before the district would be affected.[5] For the schools to lose their investment, "out of the top eight hundred companies in the world, one hundred would have to go under."[6]

As in many romances, one party seduces and the other is seduced. Noack certainly came across as a caring, considerate suitor. He started his sales drive by inviting area school administrators and board members to tea, "with food and beverage provided by Stifel Nicolaus," making the gathering seem more like a PTA fund-raiser than a high-powered investment pitch. He merely wanted to introduce the local officials to these new "AA-AAA" investments, as the invitation pointed out.

In a series of video- and audiotapes recorded by the Kenosha school board—which later joined forces with Whitefish Bay and three other nearby school districts to invest with Noack[7]—you could discern a pattern to his pitch. First he would stress the enormity of the financial problems the school districts faced in meeting their long-term retiree liabilities.[8] For example, during a seventeen-minute spiel recorded on July 24, 2006, he reminded school board members that, based on Stifel's actuarial computations, the district had an $80-million post-retiree liability. (In an "updated" Stifel study presented a year later, the estimate rose to $240 million.) In fact, Noack spent much more time describing the extent of the liability and how the district would have to account for it than he did explaining his proposed multimillion dollar investments and loans. Not to worry. He said that he had "spent the past four years" developing investment solutions for such liability problems.

Next Noack stressed that he was not about to take unacceptable risks with the schools' money. His recommended investments were extremely conservative, his approach cautious. As he put it in the July meeting, "our program . . . is using the trust to a certain degree [and] a small portion of the district's contribution, investing the money, making the spread in double-A, triple-A investments and funding a little bit at a time over a long period of time . . . and what we make is as risk-free as we can get. . . ."

He also nudged the school district along with a bit of peer-group pressure, describing how other Wisconsin districts were working with him on similar investments. There was power in numbers, he told them. By working together with other districts, they would "increase their purchasing power," a phrase he repeated many times.

Noack made it seem as if the districts' collective "purchasing power" had banks and investment houses lining up to compete for their business, offering them the lowest-cost loans and highest rates of return. He was soon going to be "bidding out" the districts' packages and he was sure he was going to get them the best rates.

To take the edge off the enormity of the investment Noack was pushing, he ended his pitch by asking the school board to pass resolutions to "authorize but not obligate" its financial committee or officials to make the investment if and when the rates seemed favorable. He never asked the boards to make a final commit-ment then and there. Instead, he conveyed the sense that even after the vote, they weren't committed to anything.

But the seduced are rarely passive. In this affair, several key board members helped the process along. On the Kenosha video-tapes, for example, one board member, Mark Hujik, a hulking, ex–Wall Street player who now owns a Wisconsin financial advisory service, repeatedly sealed the deals. The self-confident Hujik never asked a question he didn't already know the answer to. He made sure everyone knew that he knew the ins and outs of finance. At a key meeting before Kenosha signed on to its first deal, he stressed that the tens of millions in loans the board would be taking out were "moral" but not "contractual" obli-gations on behalf of the town. He implied that if things went wrong, the town really wasn't on the hook for $28.5 million in loans. (Unfortunately, he didn't mention that the town could still be successfully sued and see its debt ratings plummet if it defaulted on its "moral" financial obligations. And when a town's debt rating falls, it faces higher interest rates for all its other borrowing needs, assuming anyone will ever lend to it again.[9])

Together, Hujik and Noack wooed the parties with intimate bankerspeak that conveyed confidence and expertise. They whispered financial sweet nothings: LIBOR rates, basis points, spreads, mark to market, cost of issuance, static and managed investments, arbitrage, tranches, letters of credit, collateraliza-tion ratios, and standby-note purchase agreements. After a while the board members started using the same language. Words like "million" and "dollars" disappeared from their vocabulary; instead they referred familiarly to "twenty" and "thirty" (as in thirty million dollars). Perhaps the slang and technical lingo distracted the officials from the risky nature of their financial decisions.

Like any romance, at first everything seemed simple. There was so much trust. As one Kenosha board member said to more experienced members before a key authorization vote: "I'm not a financial person. So if you say it should be done, I will follow your lead."[10]

Listening to seven taped meetings, it's hard not to notice the school officials' consistent deference to Noack and their inability to ask him basic or troubling questions. No one wanted to seem dumb, though nearly all decidedly were not "financial persons." The district officials never asked questions such as: "How will the rate of return compare to government-guaranteed securities?" Or, "If Wall Street goes into a slump, how much could we lose?" Unless you're Woody Allen, you don't talk about the prospect of breaking up at the beginning of a romance. When the votes were taken, no one dissented.[11] Demand and Supply consummated their relationship.

To the Wisconsin school districts, the deal seemed safe. They would pool their money to increase their "purchasing power." They would borrow more money ("leverage," as the big boys call it) and invest it in something called a "synthetic CDO" for seven years. In a handout he gave to the boards on July 24, 2006, Noack illustrated how their trust fund for retirees' benefits could accumulate almost $9 million in seven years by borrowing and investing $80 million. These CDOs would pay them over 1 percent more than what it would cost to borrow the money. The more the schools borrowed, the more they would make. It was practically free money. What was not to like?

The complexity of the deal alone should have given the investors pause. Their newly purchased "Floating Rate Credit Linked Secured Notes" were a lot more complicated than federally insured CDs or treasury notes. In fact they were more convoluted than anything any of them had ever bought or sold, individually or collectively. But Noack had done his job well by making the purchases seem straightforward and prudent.

According to court documents, by the time Noack was through, the five school districts had put up $37.3 million of their own funds (most of it raised through their towns' general-obligation bonds) and borrowed $165 million more from Depfa, an aggressive Irish bank owned by a much larger German bank. The net investment after fees was $200 million. With that money, the school officials bought three different bondlike CDO financial instruments from the Royal Bank of Canada—Tribune Series 30, Sentinel Series 1, and Sentinel Series 2. With a little Wall Street magic, a big payoff seemed like a sure thing.

But what if Wall Street took a tumble and the value of the school boards' investments fell below the value of their loans? The school officials didn't even ask the question, but Noack already had the answer: "If we stick to all investment-grade companies, you still got to have ten percent . . . go under. You're talking, I would assume, and I'm not an economist, but that's a depression."[12]

The districts seemed oblivious to risk, even after securing disappointing returns on their first investments. There was a huge gap between the rates Noack had expected to lock in and what they finally got. The entire point of investing in CDOs was to get a rate of return that was substantially higher than what it would cost to borrow the money. The difference is called "the spread." Every quarter of a year you were supposed to collect what you'd earned through the spread and reinvest it. Noack had predicted that the CDOs would yield the school districts about 1.5 percent above what it would cost to borrow the money. In the first purchase, Tribune Series 30 for $25 million, the spread was 1.02 percent. However, on the next CDO purchase, Sentinel 1 for $60 million, the spread was only 0.67 percent. In their final deal, Sentinel 2 for $115 million, the spread was 0.82 percent. The idea was that after the seven years the districts could redeem their CDOs, like bonds, and have enough money to pay off the Depfa loan as well as the general-obligation bonds taken out by the town. Of course, this assumed that the CDOs would be safe and sound for seven years.

Unfortunately the CDOs were not the secure investment Noack had thought they would be. According to the *New York Times'* analysis:

> If just 6 percent of the bonds . . . went bad, the Wisconsin educators could lose all their money. If none of the bonds defaulted, the schools would receive about $1.8 million a year after paying off their own debt. By comparison, the CDO's offered only a modestly better return than a $35 million investment in ultra-safe Treasury bonds, which would have paid about $1.5 million a year, with virtually no risk.[13]

But this comparison missed the true alchemy of the deal, and its great attraction to the local school officials. Buying a safe treasury bond would have required the schools to put up $35 million from their general-obligation borrowing—money they would have to pay back and on which they would have to pay interest to the bondholders. In fact, if the districts had made such an investment, they would have had to pay *more* in interest than the treasury bonds would have yielded. That investment would make little sense.

The CDO deal was complex but it seemed to have enormous advantages: Not only would it supposedly produce $1.8 million a year in revenues, it would also pay for all the interest on the general-obligation bonds, as well as the debt itself, at the end of the seven years. That is, returns from the CDOs would cover the $165 million in loans from Depfa *and* the $35 million of collateral the schools put up through the general-obligation bonds. All in all, the deal was supposed to generate $1.8 million a year, free and clear. Now *that's* fantasy finance.

Hujik certainly had bought into the dream. "Everyone knew New York guys were making tons of money on these kinds of deals," he said. "It wasn't implausible that we could make money, too."[14]

The Wisconsin officials didn't see that their quest for this pot of gold had created two insidious problems. First, town elders were now ensnarled in a series of complicated financial transactions that yielded considerable fees for bankers and brokers. The districts paid fees to issue their general-obligation bonds; they paid fees to service those payments; they paid fees to borrow the funds to buy their CDOs; they paid fees to buy their CDOs, and they paid fees to collect the loan payments and to distribute the CDO payments. Someone would be getting rich off all this, but it wasn't the five Wisconsin school districts.

Second, when little fish try to swim with big fish, they better be prepared for risk—lots of it. No one on either side of the deal, at least on the local level, had read the fine print. They couldn't have, since the detailed documents—the "drawdown prospectuses"—were delivered weeks after the securities were purchased. They wouldn't have understood them anyway. In this romance between Supply and Demand, everyone was in over their heads. The "experts" in the room (on both sides) sounded cautious, confident, and knowledgeable. But in truth, Noack had no idea what he really was selling, and school district officials like Hujik and Yde had no idea what they really were buying. It is likely that both parties truly believed they were handling the equivalent of a mutual fund made up of highly rated corporate bonds.[15] They weren't.

It's hard to blame the Wisconsinites for not understanding the transaction: They were dealing with one of the most complex derivatives ever designed—a synthetic collateralized debt obligation, which is a combination of two other derivatives: a collateralized debt obligation (CDO) and a credit default swap (CDS). This is the kind of security that Federal Reserve chairman Ben Bernanke called "exotic and opaque." Investment guru Warren Buffet called it a "financial weapon of mass destruction."[16] In other words, one of the most dazzling—and dangerous—illusions in all of fantasy finance.

As we'll see, these investments were truly mysterious in their design and in their execution. One of the most "exotic" features was that these securities didn't give the buyer ownership of anything tangible at all. The buyer received no stake in a corporation, as they would have with a stock or bond. Instead, the school districts, without realizing it, had become part of the trillion-dollar financial insurance industry. (It was not called insurance, however, since insurance is, by law, heavily regulated.) In fact, they had put up their millions, and had borrowed millions more, to insure $20 *billion* worth of debt held (or bet upon) by the Royal Bank of Canada. And that debt included some very nasty stuff: home equity loans, leases, residential mortgage loans, commercial mortgage loans, auto finance receivables, credit card receivables, and other debt obligations.[17] Technically, Mr. Noack may have been correct when he said that the schools didn't *own* any subprime debt. *They didn't own anything.* Instead, they had agreed to *insure* junk debt. The revenue they hoped to receive each quarter was like receiving insurance premiums from the Royal Bank of Canada, which was covering its bets on the junk debt.

What's more, although the synthetic CDOs had been rated AA, as Noack had touted, those ratings were bogus. The CDOs were drawn from a vast pool of junk debt that had been chopped up into slices based on risk. The top slices had the least risk and the bottom slices had the most risk. Unbeknownst to both Noack and the school districts, the districts' $200 million of borrowed money was used to insure a slice near the bottom of the barrel! They would be on the hook for paying out claims if the default rate hit about 6 percent, a number it is fast approaching. Neither savvy Dave Noack, nor confident Mark Hujik, nor concerned Shawn Yde appeared to have any understanding of this frightening reality.

But the big fish—the CDO creators and peddlers at the top levels—knew what they were doing. The Canadian bank received $11.2 million in up-front fees. (That's right, the bank was, in effect, buying insurance, yet the school districts were paying the bank up-front fees for the honor of insuring the bank's junk debt.) The investment sales company took $1.2 million in commissions. We don't know precisely how much Depfa got for the loans, but it was substantial.

Whitefish Bay and the other school districts got something substantial too: nearly all of the risk. The school districts are about to lose all of their initial $37.3 million. They will also lose another $165 million of the money they'd borrowed from Depfa. As soon as the default rate is reached, $200 million will go to pay insurance claims to the Royal Bank of Canada. And the schools still will owe the full $165-million Depfa loan, and they will still owe on the bonds they had issued to raise much of their $37.3 million in collateral. The risk of reaching total default currently is so high that Kenosha's entire piece of the CDO investment ($35.6 million) was valued at only $925,000, as of January 29, 2009—a decline in value of $36,575,000.[18] Now the school districts are paying hefty fees not just to bankers but also to lawyers, as they sue to unwind the deal and recover damages.[19]

"This is something I'll regret until the day I die," said Shawn Yde of the Whitefish Bay schools.[20]

He's not alone. As National Public Radio and the *New York Times* reported in a joint article, "Wisconsin schools were not the only ones to jump into such complicated financial products. More than $1.2 trillion of CDOs have been sold to buyers of all kinds since 2005—including many cities and government agencies. . . ."[21]

Did these public agencies deserve any protections? A prudent rule might be to forbid investment houses to peddle such risky securities within a thousand yards of a school district. But there are no rules, since these "exotic and opaque" financial securities are still entirely unregulated. (When the Kenosha Teachers Association discovered that the securities peddled to the school districts were identical to those that sunk AIG, it requested that the Federal Reserve remove them from the school districts just as they have done for AIG—an eminently fair and reasonable request in my opinion. See chapter 8 for more on AIG.)

Whitefish Bay, Kenosha, and the other three districts made missteps and miscalculations. They were naïve. As Mark Hujik candidly said, they saw a pot of gold on Wall Street and wanted their piece. But they were had. We all were.

We know that something has gone terribly wrong not just in

Whitefish Bay but with our entire economy. There's a connection between the junk that was peddled to the "Wisconsin Five" and the crash of the global financial system. In fact, if we can understand exactly what David Noack sold to Whitefish Bay and why, we will also understand how the economy collapsed, *and* what needs to change to prevent this from happening again.

Our trail will lead to an examination of financial booms and busts, including the Great Depression. And those of us with strong stomachs will also learn more than we ever wanted to know about CDOs, CDOs-squared, synthetic CDOs, and credit default swaps—those exotic instruments that swamped Whitefish Bay.

Along the way, we will see how bankers, traders, and salespeople pocketed hundreds of millions of dollars by selling risk all over the world as if it were a collection of predictable Swiss watches. And we'll puzzle over why Alan Greenspan, Robert Rubin, and Ben Bernanke fought so hard to keep these dangerous financial instruments unregulated.

We'll tackle the "logic" of free marketeers who claim that the meltdown is the fault of low-income homebuyers who got in over their heads. We'll also marvel at how, in response to the financial meltdown, former treasury secretary Paulson and friends blew open the U.S. Treasury vault so that Wall Street could walk off with a trillion dollars . . . and counting.

And once we've put all the puzzle pieces together, we'll use our new understanding to formulate reforms that might protect us from the fantasy-finance fiasco that is harming not just Wisconsin and the rest of America, but the whole world.

| two |

The Iron Law of Fantasy Finance

THERE'S AN UNEXPECTED LINK between the richest residents of Whitefish Bay and the financial toxic waste that came back to haunt them. That story starts in the early 1970s, when something strange happened to our economy: An iron law of economics melted down.

At that time, I was trudging through graduate school, where I learned that workers' wages (that is, "real" wages, after accounting for inflation) are tied to labor's productivity—output per hour worked. Our professors all but rapped our knuckles as they drilled it in: Productivity and real wages are two sides of a coin, forever joined. As workers produce more goods and services per hour (that is, increase their productivity), their wages *must* rise. Why? Because as productivity rises, firms will increase profits by seeking more workers, which in turn bids up the price of labor. My microeconomics teachers even argued that other forces, like collective bargaining, really can't change this relationship. For instance, if unions push wages up faster than productivity, either inflation will kick in, bringing real wages back down, or employers will start laying people off, increasing the supply of labor and reducing its price.

So went the theory, and the proof was right before our eyes in the post–World War II productivity-and-wage data. As output per worker-hour went up, average workers' real wages rose in tandem. They tracked nearly perfectly, year after year.

As the United States battled the communists for ideological supremacy, this iron law highlighted the economic might and inherent justice of American capitalism. Output per worker just kept rising, and the economy just kept growing, as measured by gross domestic product (GDP)—the value of all our goods and services. And as workers' real wages rose, the average working family could buy more of the goods and services they produced. Our standard of living grew more steadily and faster than anywhere else on earth. In short, the iron law of economics I learned in grad school was the foundation of the American dream. Year after year things would get better for those who worked hard and played by the rules of free enterprise. Each generation would do better than the previous one.

And then, suddenly, everything changed. Productivity and wages, American workers discovered, weren't inextricably linked after all. Starting in the mid 1970s, productivity was still rising— sometimes slowly, sometimes quickly, for a total increase of 94 percent in the past three decades. But wages went flat beginning in 1973, and they are still flat or declining today.

The average nonsupervisory worker actually earned *more* in 1973 than today, in real (inflation-adjusted) dollars. Consider chart 2, which shows what real weekly wages would have been had they continued to rise in lockstep with productivity. (The

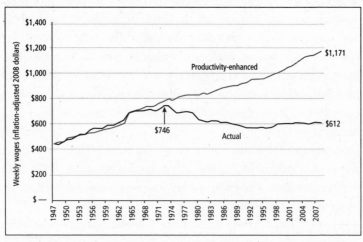

Chart 2. Actual Wages vs. Productivity-Enhanced Wages in the United States. Author's calculations using Bureau of Labor Statistics data

top line is the productivity index converted into wages and so is called productivity-enhanced wages.) The two lines are snugly aligned from 1947 to about 1973. Then they diverge as average real wages stall and then decline.

By 2007, real wages (in today's dollars) had slid from their peak of $746 per week in 1973 to $612 per week—an 18 percent drop. Had wages increased along with productivity, the current average real wage for nonsupervisory workers would be $1,171 per week—$60,892 per year instead of today's average of $31,824.

Consider the implications. Although their wages stopped rising, workers were getting more and more productive with each hour they worked. As a result, the economy was growing, with ever more goods and services produced per worker-hour. The money value of those goods and services had to go somewhere. Clearly workers didn't take that money home. So who did?

Maybe that mysteriously disappearing productivity bonus went to pay for our benefits—like health care. We know health care costs have shot up. Is that where our lost wage increases went?

No, not according to the numbers. Chart 3 tracks real hourly *total* compensation for all workers (except farmers)—which includes every employee cost borne by the employer—wages, pensions, health care, vacations, paid leave, unemployment insurance, disability, and Social Security. As is clear, that telltale post-1973 gap between wages and productivity is still there. Our average real hourly compensation is now about $25 per hour including all benefits, representing a small increase from the early 1970s. If it had risen along with productivity, it would be more like $41 an hour. The productivity bonus—about $16 per hour—is still AWOL.

I'm sure you've guessed where it went: Nearly all of it was snatched by the owners of capital—the wealthiest of the "investment class." In 1973 the top 1 percent of earners took in 8 percent of the nation's total income. By 2006, the top 1 percent got nearly 23 percent of the pie, the highest proportion since 1929.[1]

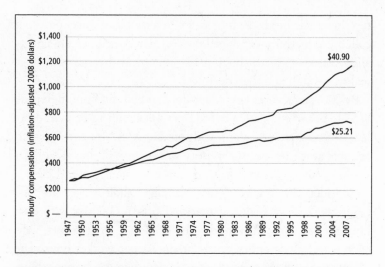

Chart 3. Real Hourly Total Compensation vs. Productivity, U.S. Non-farm Business Sector 1947–2008 (3rd Q). Author's calculations using Bureau of Labor Statistics data

As real wages stalled, more and more families relied on two wage earners to make ends meet. Between the addition of a second wage earner, the addition of second jobs for individual wage earners, and working longer hours, the average married couple increased their total number of hours worked per year by 25 percent from 1950 to 2005.[2] Nevertheless, as chart 4 shows, even with that increase in work time, household income for working people rose modestly over the past twenty-five years, or not at all. Clearly our productivity gains have found their way into the pockets of the wealthy, like those who live in Whitefish Bay's shoreline mansions.

There are 94 million nonsupervisory workers out there who are not getting their fair share of the spoils of their increased productivity. An estimate for just the most current year—*one year*—of the gap between what workers should have gotten and what they actually received (in wages and benefits) is a staggering $3 trillion—equivalent to about $32,000 per worker in the United States. Most of that money went instead to the investor class all over the world.

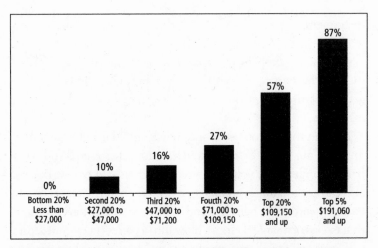

Chart 4. Change in Real Family Income by Quintile and Top Five Percent, 1979–2006. U.S. Census Bureau, Historical Income Tables, F1, F3

And what exactly did those rich investors do with our money? They spent some of it on themselves, to be sure. But even they can only buy so many houses, cars, and jets. In fact, the rich invested most of this unearned bonus. (It always feels better to have your money make money—and *then* spend it.)

Some of the money was invested in old-fashioned places like factories, or even in newfangled start-ups. But there was so much money roaming the globe that it ran out of "real" economy investments. Instead, much of this massive surplus found its way into high finance. Investors here and around the globe stocked up on some very fancy financial instruments that had only a tenuous relationship with the brick-and-mortar economy.

Imagine that "real" economic production of tangible goods and services takes place on the surface of the earth. And imagine that finance is the atmosphere—the clouds and the air that allow our real earthly economic entities to breathe and grow through loans and other access to capital. This financial atmosphere is directly connected to real production, because all loans are claims on the real assets of the global economy. The financial "air" is made of financial markets (often called capital markets) and financial instruments (stocks, bonds, etc.) that move capital from those who have it to those who need it—at least in theory. The financial air brings cash to enterprises that require it. New companies get the start-up money they need; businesses and consumers get credit to buy goods and services that they couldn't afford otherwise.

To run properly, our economy needs just the right amount of financial air. If there's not enough, banks choke up. And when banks stop lending, you get a financial crisis—like now. But you also can get too much financial air—more than the real economy back on earth can handle. And when the conditions are right, that excess of financial air can blow into a perfect economic storm.

If we sum up all the productivity bonuses workers haven't gotten since 1973, it's easy to see how the financial skies would be filling with clouds of capital looking for a home. While some of that money was productively invested in the real global economy, trillions of dollars of *surplus capital* found its way into the fantasy-finance casino. Here's how *Wall Street Journal* reporters Greg Ip and Mark Whitehouse put it in 2005:

> There's an unprecedented wave of capital flowing around the world, with all of its owners anxiously searching for a better return. World pension, insurance and mutual funds have $46 trillion at their disposal, up almost a third from 2000. . . .
>
> The result is that global investors are diving into a wide range of riskier assets: emerging countries' stocks and bonds; real estate and real-estate-backed debt; commodity funds; fine art; private-equity funds, which buy stakes in nonpublic companies; and the investment contracts called derivatives, including a kind structured to permit the sophisticated to take huge bond risks.[3]

To suck up this surplus capital, the financial sector invented scores of spanking new financial instruments for the wealthy to

buy. Just a few years later, those deliciously high-yielding investments turned into financial toxic waste, plunging our economy
into a deep and dangerous recession.

The story gets stranger still. As Wall Street soared on the wings
of its great new financial instruments, more money became available for loans . . . to working people. And workers, whose wages
had dragged for decades because they didn't get their productivity bonuses, really racked up the debt—in the form of mortgages,
credit card debt, auto and student loans. *We were borrowing back
our own money!*

Chart 5 shows the rise of our indebtedness. From about 1960 to
1985, at any one moment in time, we owed about $0.60 for every
dollar we earned in a year (after taxes). But as the productivity-
wage gap widened, we started to borrow more and more. As of
2006, we owed $1.27 for every dollar we earned.

To jump ahead in our story a bit, this ever-rising level of household debt was unsustainable. There's a finite limit to how much
debt working people could take on to buy more and more goods
and services. When they hit the wall, consumer demand crashed
and the economy suffered.

But that's not the main reason our economy took a nosedive.

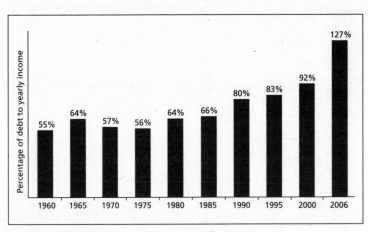

Chart 5. Household Debt-to-Income Ratio in the United States. Federal Reserve
Board and Bureau of Economic Analysis data from www.demographia.com/#econ

Far from it. In fact, a good deal of the surplus capital the wealthy skimmed from us *did not* get recycled back to us as debt. No, much of it went into the fantasy finance casino and turned into bets, just like the ones that were pawned off on the Wisconsin school districts. Our story is about how those new financial investments were created and how they turned toxic, crashing the financial sector and then the rest of the economy.

In honor of Whitefish Bay, I propose a new iron law of economics very different from the one I learned in graduate school. It goes something like this: When we allow surplus capital to pile up in the hands of the few, the money will be pumped into a fantasy-finance casino that will ultimately crash the economy. And here's the unfortunate corollary: When that casino goes bust, we pay yet again—in lost jobs and pensions—and in tax dollars to bail out the biggest financial institutions that crashed the system in the first place.

We'll save for chapter 11 what caused wages and productivity to split apart in the early 1970s, and how to narrow the gap. But first, we'll take a closer look at all this financial "innovation." Is it socially useful or just sophisticated roulette?

| three |

Is There a Dime's Bit of Difference between Wall Street's "Innovation" and Gambling?

THE WISCONSIN FIVE wanted their money to beget money. Actually, they wanted *borrowed* money to do all the begetting. There is a very long and controversial history about whether or not that's a good thing.

Money seems to have sprung up about 9,000 years ago. The first currency was cows. Before we developed crops, our ancestors domesticated wild animals. A few of these species (taurine and zebu) became cattle that provided people with food, milk, and a way to carry loads.

Apparently, from the start, *Homo sapiens* has had a fondness for trading just about everything. We loved to barter. If we had a little extra of something, we wanted to trade it for stuff we didn't have. But as our societies became more complex, it became increasingly cumbersome to work out the exact terms of each barter deal. So items were measured against the value of a cow. One cow equals so many spears or concubines.

The Chinese were the first to figure out that coinlike objects might be easier to put in your purse than a cow. They started using cowry shells—those shiny porcelain-like sea shells that were easily carried and transferred. Their beauty also gave them intrinsic value. In Africa, cowry shells were also known for their magical powers and were associated with fertility.

Herodotus, the ancient Greek historian, noted that by 687 B.C., the kingdom of Lydia (in what is now western Turkey) used minted coins. Historians believe this might have been the first society to systematically do so. In short order, decorative metals—silver and gold—became the standard means of exchange.

People were probably long familiar with loans: I will give you my extra cow now, and you will give me back a cow later. Or maybe you will give me back an armful of wheat every new moon for twelve new moons. But at some point—historians don't know exactly when—people came up with the idea of charging interest: You can have my extra cow now, but only if you give me a cow back next year plus an armful of wheat every month. (Interest may have started because animals could reproduce during the period of the loan. Who got the calf?)

Early on, our hard-working ancestors worried about the impact on society of those who received extra wealth from loans. Money lenders often were viewed as leeching off those who worked hard for their bread. Long before Christ, people were making a clear distinction between earned and unearned income. But more importantly, they worried about the consequences for the community: The indebted could become slaves to their creditors, and destabilize the social order.

The concept of interest was first codified about 4,500 years ago in Mesopotamia, as that society developed an urban civilization that relied on a division of labor. Wheat growers, fishermen, and herders in the countryside fed the urban population of craftsmen, priests, and government officials. The temple, and later the central government, took in surpluses from the countryside (taxes in the form of agricultural produce) and distributed the goods to the urban dwellers. Everyone had to pay some kind of tribute (taxes) to the temple and the state. If you couldn't pay, you borrowed either from others or from the central government to cover what you owed.

King Hammurabi (1790–52 B.C.), whose administration was the first to use writing to codify his decrees, allowed interest to be paid on loans of barley and silver. We have records of these loans. For example, "Igizi, the blacksmith" owed 720 liters of barley. So did "Kikuli, the shepherd" and "Ur-Hamazida, the plowman."[1] There were also loans made by individuals to other individuals. The loans often were needed to cover harvest short-falls. Sometimes they were needed to purchase bridal gifts as well. Loans seemed ubiquitous and formed the bulk of the written record. And many of these written loan agreements contained provisions for interest. The fact that so much of the early written record was dedicated to financial transactions and laws suggests that the stability of the social order required that finance be care-fully controlled.

It seems that Hammurabi and his advisors—as well as his subjects—understood that loans, especially at high interest rates, could enslave the poor and make the lender excessively rich. Therefore, his codes limited interest rates: 33.3 percent if you loaned barley and 20 percent for silver loans. (This was for the life of the loan, not per year. So for short-term loans this was a very high rate.) The codes also forgave loans in case of natural disasters, literally wiping the slate clean, at least if the loan was recorded: "If anyone owes a debt for a loan, and a storm pros-trates the grain, or the harvest fail, or the grain does not grow for lack of water; in that year he need not give his creditor any grain, he washes his debt-tablet in water and pays no rent for this year."[2]

The Greeks, however, were far less supportive of the idea of interest. Aristotle thought it unnatural and therefore unethical:

> The most hated sort and with the greatest reason, is usury which makes a gain out of money itself and nor from the natural object of it. For money was intended to be used in exchange but not to increase at interest. And this term interest, which means the birth of money from money is applied to the breeding of money because the offspring resembles the parent. Wherefore of all modes of getting wealth, this is the most unnatural.[3]

In his *Ethics*, Aristotle put money lenders in with a bad crowd, namely "those who ply sordid trades, pimps and all such people and those who lend sums at high rates. For all these take more than they ought, and from the wrong sources. What is common to them is evidently a sordid love of gain. . . ."[4]

Many Greek and Roman philosophers agreed. Republican Rome in 340 B.C. outlawed interest entirely.

It appears that every society and culture that has used some form of money has struggled with the notion of interest and excessive interest payments. None more so than the Jewish people. In fact, the Hebrew word for interest is *neshekh*, meaning "a bite." In the Talmud and other rabbinical texts, it was generally agreed that no interest at all should be charged to fellow Jews. But it was okay to charge interest on loans to Gentiles, because they charged *you* interest. Rabbinical scholars also were acutely aware that there were hundreds of ways to beat the system, including bringing a Gentile into the mix so that interest on a loan could be laundered through a third party. However, they were very concerned that charging interest could victimize the poor. And they were even more worried that compound interest (adding accumulated interest back to the principal so that the lender earns interest on their interest) would create more misery.

The Prophet Muhammad (in about A.D. 600) and the Koran took a harder line: No interest at all was permitted. "And what you give in interest that it may increase on (other) people's wealth, increases not with Allah . . ." (Koran 30:39).[5] (This stricture is still followed by some banks in Islamic countries.)

For nearly a thousand years the Catholic Church also weighed in heavily against all forms of interest. First the clergy were prohibited from charging interest, then the laity. In 1311, Pope Clement V declared all secular laws that allowed interest null and void.

But a much more complicated reality grew up between church and state. Kings needed someone to finance commerce and war. Who could do it? It was very risky for Catholics to loan money, since they could be excommunicated for usury. How about the Jews? (Actually, any non-Christian minority would do.) At the height of the Middle Ages, when the church ban was strongest, sovereigns encouraged specific Jewish merchants to go into the money trade. The Jewish money traders were permitted, even encouraged, to charge high interest rates. But there was a catch: The sovereign could and did seize the wealth accumulated by the Jewish lenders either during their lives or upon their deaths. According to the Jewishencyclopedia.com, "It was for this reason indeed that the kings supported the Jews, and even objected to their becoming Christians, because in that case they could not have forced from them money won by usury. Thus both in England and in France the kings demanded to be compensated [by the Church] for every Jew converted."[6]

As commercialization accelerated, church bans on usury faded, and all manner of Catholic lenders entered the field. Nevertheless, the caricature of the Jewish money lender persisted. While the Protestant Reformation's famous "work ethic" helped fuel the rise of commerce, the man who officially launched the Reformation, Martin Luther, railed against the concept of interest. In *Trading and Usury* (1524), Luther wrote, "He who lends expecting to get back something more or something better than he has loaned, is clearly a damned usurer, since even those who lend demanding or expecting to get back just what they have lent, and taking no risk of its return, are not acting in a Christian way."[7]

John Calvin, however, pulled away from the severe Catholic and Lutheran restrictions on interest lending. As inflation of currencies became more common, Calvin apparently was among the first theologians to understand that money lent today might be paid back with money worth less in the future owing to inflation. Therefore, the lender needed interest payments just to break even. But Calvin still wanted restrictions on the practice. For example, he argued that it was morally just to lend money for commercial trading only if the risks were borne both by lender and borrower. If the ship went down both should lose, rather than having the lender repaid regardless of outcome. This theological change corresponded with the dramatic rise of international trade as sailing ships improved and the Europeans colonized the globe.

As the commercial world became more complex so did the role of finance. Interest was here to stay. But for the sake of society's well-being, the first political economists worried about how much it should be controlled. Adam Smith, the foremost theorist of capitalism, tried to bring sound economic reason to the issue of interest. He wanted the most productive deployment of capital. It was okay, he argued, to borrow money and pay the going interest rate *if* the money was used productively. But Smith deplored the idea of aristocratic profligates securing loans to buy goodies for themselves. Instead, he wanted borrowed money to be invested in productive enterprises that would make the investor a profit, employ more citizens, and generally add to the wealth of the nation. Although Smith believed usury could pose a problem, the solution was not to forbid lenders from charging interest. That, he believed, would only drive the citizenry deeper into the arms of unsavory usurers: "This regulation, instead of preventing, has been found from experience to increase the evil of usury; the debtor being obliged to pay not only for the use of the money, but for the risk his creditor runs . . . to insure his creditor from the penalties of usury."[8]

Smith may have conjured up the idea of "the invisible hand" of the market, but he thought the government should have a hand too—at least when it came to usury. He argued that the government should cap interest rates at just above the rate that the market was charging prime borrowers (those with the best prospects of repaying because of their assets and incomes). Why so low? Because, he wrote, with high interest rates, "a great part of the capital of the country would thus be kept out of the hands which were most likely to make a profitable and advantageous use of it, and thrown into those which were most likely to waste and destroy it."[9] With a ceiling on interest rates, a lender would

not want to risk loaning money to those (subprime) wasteful aris-
tocrats who would surely gamble and drink it away.

Karl Marx went one step further. He believed that banking,
interest, and credit created an illusionary and unstable world of
fantasy finance. In 1867, he observed:

> With the development of interest-bearing capital and
> the credit system, all capital seems to double itself, and
> sometimes treble itself, by the various modes in which
> the same capital, or perhaps even the same claim on a
> debt, appears in different forms in different hands. The
> greater portion of this "money-capital" is purely ficti-
> tious. All the deposits, with the exception of the reserve
> fund, are merely claims on the banker, which, however,
> never exist as deposits.[10]

In short, it seems that everyone everywhere in every era—from
Hammurabi to Aristotle to Adam Smith to Karl Marx; from
the Greeks to the Jews to the Muslims to the Christians—has
understood that finance—money-making-money—poses serious
difficulties for the social order. We are painfully relearning these
lessons.

———

Does high finance still threaten the social order? The answer has
little to do with individual greed or morality. Rather we need to
understand how financial markets break down modern economies. The leading issue is systemic risk—losses that don't merely
harm individual investors or firms, but can undermine the functioning of the entire economy.

Until very recently, too many of our economic leaders and
academics believed that such risk had been drastically curtailed,
if not forever eliminated. The modern financial sector could do
no wrong. Policy makers and economists lavished unqualified
praise on the industry's innovative new financial products, which

fueled the sector's huge growth and attracted capital from all over the world. Now these same products are commonly called "toxic waste," and the financial industry called a "casino." So—is the industry a cauldron of innovation or a superfund site? Are these new products the financial sector's equivalent of the iPod? Or lead paint and asbestos?

Consider for a moment your home. Without a financial instrument—the mortgage—very few of us could afford to purchase a home. We need credit and we need the payments spread out over many years. The same goes for those who start new enterprises or expand existing ones. In general, credit fuels economic growth and keeps enterprises moving. And what those with capital love most about the financial industry is that all these good things happen simply because the industry is looking to maximize its own returns, like any other enterprise. Money-making-money doesn't care about jobs or housing or the common good. Smith's invisible hand translates this innate selfishness into national well-being. (One evening after soccer practice I had a conversation with a private equity manager, a fellow soccer dad in my town. I was trying to get him to talk about the social utility of his work, so I asked him how his investments helped businesses expand and create jobs. He turned to me with his big, infectious smile and said, "Les, I'm in it for the money.")

But . . . if the invisible hand is doing its job, why is it so hard to identify the many wonderful new products the financial sector has created? Innovations that have improved our world, fulfilled a need? These money-making-money instruments must be playing an important economic role. If they were just props in an elaborate game of fantasy finance, surely they would not endure. Would they?

John Kay, writing in the *Financial Times*, refers to the financial sector as "a utility attached to a casino. The utility is the payments system that enables individuals and non-financial companies to go about their everyday business confident that they can make or receive payments, and lend and borrow to finance normal transactions." The casino is, well, a casino where tens of thousands of very bright people try to beat the odds. [11]

Kay believes you can't have one without the other, and that the casino part is that cauldron of financial innovation. In fact he argues that it is folly to try to control or eliminate the casino since the industry will always invent new ways to work around regulations. So if you want a robust financial system, says Kay, you must accept the casino's innovation.

But if Kay is right—and we better hope he's not—what *are* those wonderful innovations, exactly?

Here's one: the pawnshop. It debuted in a monastery in China in A.D. 662—or at least that's the earliest record, thanks to a pawn book that survived the centuries. The idea was simple: You give me something of value and I give you money (originally in the form of gold or silver). When you give me the money back, I give you back the item. From the monastery, the concept spread, at first to a Chinese princess, who supplemented her income through a pawn business. About eight hundred years later the Franciscans in Italy tried the very same idea. According to historians Valerie Hansen and Ana Mata-Fink, these pawnshops had "the explicit goal of giving ordinary people an alternative to usurers . . . Like Chinese monasteries, they initially did not charge interest."[12]

It was only a small step to turn the pawnshop into a bank that would loan out money against a pledge of collateral. Add interest and the relending of deposits to the mix and you've got the makings of a very powerful and profitable institution.

An interest-bearing pawnshop loan, however, was clunky when all you could loan out was gold and silver. The Chinese fixed that problem with the next great financial invention—paper money. They figured that money didn't need to be a precious metal or a valuable cow. It didn't need to have any intrinsic value at all. In the tenth century A.D., after the Song dynasty had unified a large part of the country, the economy was humming. Gold and silver, which were used as currency, started to disappear as external trade expanded. Soon businesses began using cheaper metals like bronze and finally abundant iron.[13] Carting all that iron to market was extremely cumbersome. So a few clever merchants came up with the paper bill. By 1024 the state stepped in and created the first official paper currency, controlling the amount and guaranteeing its value.

Really, this is quite a feat. That a worthless piece of paper serves as a means of exchange still boggles the mind. You pull this scrap of nothing out of your pocket and someone gives you a latte—all because the government says it is worth much more than the paper it is printed on. It truly is faith-based currency. (And with our current technology, electronic money will make paper money practically disappear as it is reduced to nothing more than electronic impulses.)

So far we have the financial innovations of the pawnshop (bank) and paper money. Somehow these inventions don't inspire the same awe we feel for the printing press or the light bulb. But let's not call the question just yet.

As trade evolved in Europe, a truly momentous innovation evolved with it—a functioning capital market. Here, money could be raised for all kinds of ventures, primarily through the buying and selling of financial instruments (which we'll describe below). This innovation gives our financial sector major bragging rights, because it enabled people to raise capital for ventures (including wars) that could expand economic activity and state power. Financial experts are quick to remind us that capital markets provide the venture capital that is absolutely vital for developing new products and services. No capital markets, no high-speed Internet, no laptop computers, no Prozac.

Two prior innovations came together to produce functioning capital markets. The first was government bonds. The first real public-debt bonds that could be bought and sold were issued by Italy's city-states, which had wracked up big debts in their wars with each other and other Mediterranean nations. (In fact, war has usually been the driver for government debt.) Venice,

Genoa, and Florence needed money, but they'd already taxed their citizens to the hilt. So they hit upon a much bigger and better idea—sell people bonds and pay them interest. At first the city-states made buying such bonds compulsory. Then they realized that they could attract money from their wealthiest citizens simply by issuing government-backed debt and selling it. They could spread out interest payments to only a few times a year, which made the arrangement very affordable. Large sums could be raised quickly. Creditors could buy the bonds, and, most importantly, they could resell them to each other. By the late 1400s, all three city-states were circulating some form of negotiable government debt instrument. The bonds not only raised cash for war, but literally bonded the wealthy to the state. Everyone who owned a piece of the government debt had a tangible stake in the government's well-being.

While Italy produced the first transferable government bonds, it didn't develop the other ingredient necessary to produce a fully fledged capital market: corporate shareholders. The Dutch East India Company, founded in 1602, became the first to offer shares. The corporation was organized by the Dutch state to systematize the hundreds of sailing ventures from competing Dutch port cities to the Far East. By issuing shares, the company provided a piece of the action to each of its participants. The company was controlled by a board of directors that included representatives from each of the cities involved. Amsterdam, the largest, received the most directors. At first the shares (legal documents that described the buyer's ownership) were only redeemable by the company. Later, a secondary market grew up to buy and sell shares.

This buying and selling of shares in the Dutch East India Company became the basis of the first stock market. Not only could the shares be sold, they also could be used as collateral for loans to fund other ventures. This gave rise to all manner of modern financial transactions. The company's sailing ventures were a gamble. Profits and therefore dividends were in no way guaranteed, nor was the timing of payments. Before long, some innovative soul realized that it might make sense to exchange shares in the future based on a price agreed upon in the present.

Such a futures transaction was a hedge against uncertainty. It would lock in money for the holder of the shares, while allowing the buyer a chance to make a bit more in the future when the dividends rolled in. The practice of locking in future prices also helped protect the share price of those who had pledged their shares as loan collateral.[14]

Although this Dutch stock market thrived, the first fully fledged capital market was born in seventeenth-century England. For the next two hundred years, England was the hub of the world's financial market. England had both necessary ingredients: government debt and the shareholder corporation. The British parliament chartered the Bank of England in 1694 to raise money for accumulated debts. Bonds were sold to the public, and the debt was readily transferable. Meanwhile, investors chartered the West India Company, a shareholder-driven rival to the Dutch. Companies sprang up right and left to raise cash for new ventures—especially for dredging up wrecks that supposedly were laden with riches. Diving and dredging companies were all the rage in England. Although most of these companies failed, they helped create a flourishing capital market. At the market, investors could buy and sell existing shares and debt, and entrepreneurs could raise money (by selling new shares) for new ventures.

Government debt, the shareholder corporation, and a capital market were each world-changing inventions, the financial equivalent of electricity.

But before we get too euphoric about these breakthroughs, we need to take a look at the troublesome twins spawned by these new capital markets—the bubble and the bust. Enter systemic risk. Long before there was Wall Street, there was the bubble. Something about the financial market seems to encourage financial booms, which lead to bubbles, which lead to debilitating financial collapses. Only the blindest ideologue could ignore the historical connection between financial panics and "free" financial markets. When left to their own devices, financial markets always melt down, eventually. (Scholars have counted 148 meltdowns since 1870 where a country's economy has shrunk by 10 percent or more. They also found 87 instances where per-person consumption dropped by that amount. On average the size of the drop was 21 to 22 percent and lasted three and a half years.[15])

The first sizable bubble and bust involved the tulip-loving Dutch during the 1630s, a time of commercial success and relative peace. Thriving regional trade had enabled Dutch merchants to accumulate significant wealth and enough surplus income to indulge in conspicuous consumption. The Dutch adored rare varieties of tulips for their beauty and because they advertised the wealth of those who possessed them. According to financial historian Edward Chancellor, "In 1624, a Semper Augustus[16] fetched the handsome sum of 1,200 florins, an amount sufficient to purchase a small Amsterdam town house."[17] Soon nearly all tulip varieties were in high demand, generating a vibrant tulip-trading market. But this was not your typical floral market. Since tulips could only be grown at certain times of the year, the market developed contracts for future delivery, secured by borrowed money. As a result, "most transactions were for tulip bulbs that could never be delivered because they didn't exist and were paid for with credit notes that could never be honored because the money wasn't there."[18] This practice of leveraging (buying stuff with lots of borrowed money) drove up prices to insane levels: One Viceroy tulip bulb was supposedly worth the equivalent of "twenty-seven tons of wheat, fifty tons of rye, four fat oxen, eight fat pigs, twelve fat sheep, two hogsheads of wine, four turns of beer, two tons of butter, three tons of cheese, a bed with linen, a wardrobe of clothes and a silver beaker."[19] As prices climbed, word spread, attracting more and more of the Dutch as well as foreign investors into the market—further inflating prices. For a short time it seemed that small and large fortunes came to those who bought and sold tulip contracts. Modest tradesmen got into the act by taking out loans against their homes and other assets. The casino was open for almost a year and it seemed that everyone came away a winner.

No one is sure why the crash came on that day, February 3, 1637. Prices plummeted so catastrophically that a year later a government commission had to unwind the tulip contracts altogether, declaring that each could be annulled on payment of only 3.5 percent of the agreed price. Although the Dutch economy did not collapse, a great many players were badly burned. The Dutch love of tulips turned to disgust.

We've had nearly four hundred years to absorb the lesson of this market bubble. And yet we haven't. Obviously, we are prone to get-rich schemes. We move like a herd when the chase is on for items of apparent value. The more others move, the more we want in on the action. As share prices rocket upward, we want to get our piece, further driving up the price. Then, at the moment when the gap between the intrinsic worth of the item and reality stretches to the breaking point, the herd stampedes in the other direction. Prices reverse, leading to more selling, and an even more swooping decline. Because so much of the upside is fueled by borrowed money, the downside accelerates when the collateral for the loans—the shares that were bought—declines in value. Shares then must be sold to pay off the loans and a death spiral follows: declining share prices leads to more sales to repay loans, which leads to more declining prices. Nearly four centuries later, then Federal Reserve chairman Alan Greenspan called the upside "irrational exuberance."[20]

The Dutch Tulip Bubble was harmless compared to the bubbles that followed. England's South Sea Bubble of 1720 more accurately foretold our financial future.

The South Sea Corporation was founded to conduct trade and to market much of the English national debt, which was until then held by wealthy citizens in the form of annuities.[21] The corporation encouraged these rich annuity holders to convert their holdings into South Sea Corporation shares, which would pay dividends. In the process, the government's debt would disappear, and a new secondary market would be created that would allow the wealthy annuity holders to unload their assets more readily. The new company cut a careful deal with the Bank of England: The higher the price of the shares, the higher the profits for the investors. In fact, higher share prices benefited the government by making it more tempting for annuity holders to convert their claims on the government into corporate shares. To grease the skids, many members of Parliament were given stock, as were various cabinet ministers. The stock soon became wildly popular, and the bubble began to expand. In only six months the stock's value increased eight times its original price. The euphoria spread throughout the growing English capital market, leading to a profusion of new bubble companies seeking—and finding—investors for fraudulent ventures.

The South Sea corporate directors didn't like all these imitators entering the frothing market in search of sterling and suckers. They wanted the government to tamp down the proliferation of these competing bubble companies by requiring all new shareholder corporations to get a government charter. The "Bubble Act" barred "the establishment of companies without parliamentary permission and prevented existing companies from carrying on activities not specified by their charters."[22] When this failed to suppress the bubble companies, the South Sea directors asked the attorney general to prosecute. They also increased the company's guaranteed dividend to a whopping 50 percent per year for the next twelve years to get the attention of investors who were chasing after high returns in the boom market. The combination of government regulation plus the exorbitant dividend was supposed to further drive up stocks. Instead, the euphoric stock market crashed, taking down the South Sea enterprise with it. In four weeks the value of South Sea's stock fell by 75 percent.

In the decades and centuries to come, such bubbles would form and burst again and again—from South American mines, to railroads, to the stock market bubble of the 1920s, to the crash of the Internet and housing bubbles in the early twenty-first century. Investors can't help themselves, nor can the financial system as a whole. The key players always find ways to profit wildly by building the momentum and pumping up prices well past any reasonable value. The process of borrowing to buy more assets and the inflation of those asset prices reinforce each other. At some point, the gap between fantasy finance and reality stretches to the snapping point. And then comes the collapse. Sometimes, the underlying economy is strong and the impact is contained. At other times, the collapse sets off a deep depression that threatens the entire economy.

We've examined some important financial inventions: government bonds, shareholders, capital markets, with their inevitable bubbles and busts. But we've missed the financial market's greatest invention of all: *political leverage*. Big investors and other major financial players have become so strong that they are almost impossible to control effectively by government policies. Put more bluntly, high finance reigns, or at least has exorbitant veto power over economic and political life. (Note how today's politicians respond to the gyrations of the stock market.)

Take the South Sea Bubble. After the bubble burst, government investigators discovered that many members of Parliament had been bought off with valuable shares. Several were expelled from their seats. In fact, Parliament went so far as to pass a bill to confiscate all the profits made by the South Sea Company directors during 1720. It never was implemented. Remarkably, in the 1820s, the Bubble Act was actually removed from the books after yet another finance bubble. This time the bubble concerned fantasy gold and silver mines in South America. British investors believed that South America, which recently had liberated itself from Spanish rule, would benefit greatly from English know-how and commerce. Surely once the English got involved with these South American mines, money would flow to the investors. British publications touted the humongous gold nuggets that were just lying on the ground, waiting to be processed by British companies. All those companies—and the emerging South American governments—needed were some wise English investors. The binge was on. Company after company floated shares. Markets and prices were effectively manipulated, spurious investment reports were circulated, and government ministers were turned into cheerleaders with free shares. Prices took off . . . and then crashed.

By this time some English observers had already seen enough to question the fundamental value of the financial markets and those who made them tick (and manipulated them). These observers had noticed how these markets resembled a casino. One banking family scion, Alexander Baring, said that he "saw no difference between the gambling of the nobleman in the halls of St. James's Street, and the gambling of the merchant on the Royal Exchange; except that the latter kept earlier hours and more respectable company than the former."[23]

Even though the financial markets were rife with fraudulent manipulation, the English government refused to act. Why? Enter the innovation of financial political leverage and power. By this time the financial markets had become inexorably attached to the ideology of the "free market," a horse they would ride to riches for the next two hundred years. They had convinced political rulers that unregulated financial markets, though messy, were the heartbeat of capitalism. And these markets could not—and should not—be constrained or even seriously controlled. In essence, financiers argued that it was impossible to draw a line between healthy speculation and venal overspeculation without killing the market. You could not really differentiate a bubble from legitimate investment until after the fact. Alexander Baring put it well in 1820:

The evil [of speculators] was certainly one which deserved
to be checked; though he hardly knew how the check
could be applied. The remedy would be worse than the
disease, if in putting a stop to this evil, they put a stop to
the spirit of enterprise. That spirit was productive of so
much benefit to the community, that he should be sorry
to see any person drawing a line, discriminating between
fair enterprise and extravagant speculation.[24]

This argument has been trotted out for nearly two centuries to
protect the financial markets from effective regulations, and to
condone "irrational exuberance." When major financial players
fear a government policy or regulation, they threaten calamity.
Nearly always, politicians of all stripes back them up. Political
leaders live in fear of how the "markets" will respond to their
statements and policies. A strong market decline after a policy
pronouncement is nearly the equivalent of a parliamentary vote
of no-confidence.

Or as President Bill Clinton put it: "You mean to tell me that
the success of the economic program and my re-election hinges
on the Federal Reserve and a bunch of fucking bond traders?"[25]

four

Learning and Unlearning the Lessons of the Great Depression

As THE WISCONSIN SCHOOL DISTRICTS found out the hard way, banks and brokers can sell you dubious financial securities with little or no government oversight. This is not an accident. Financial institutions, in fact, are very good at resisting and undermining regulatory control. But sometimes by avoiding regulation, they create the conditions for their own meltdown.

As we've seen, the boom-and-bust cycle is a regular feature of our economic system. Major financial players seem to thrive with these gyrations, so long as they aren't too extreme. But in the absence of controls, the ups and downs can be cataclysmic. What if the bust is so deep that the entire economy collapses? Suddenly the ideology of deregulation gets tossed under the bus by even the staunchest of free-market advocates. This is precisely what happened during the Great Depression and is happening again in our current crisis.

We need to take a closer look at the Great Depression for several reasons. First, we may be heading there again. Second, in the 1930s our government enacted serious financial controls that for decades managed to put the kibosh on fantasy finance. And finally, scholars and policy makers are tackling today's financial crisis with lessons gleaned from the Great Depression. In fact, Federal Reserve chief Ben Bernanke, formerly a professor at Princeton, is a leading Great Depression scholar, and he views the current financial crisis through that prism. As Bernanke puts it, "I am a Great Depression buff, the way some people are Civil War buffs."[1]

By the time of the 1929 crash, the prevailing ideology was Social Darwinism (the survival of the fittest) fused with a laissez-faire approach to government. The boom-and-bust cycle was sometimes painful, but necessary—a way for capitalism to cleanse itself by getting rid of the weaker companies, taming labor, and thereby increasing overall efficiency and productivity. The strong would survive, prosper . . . and rule. This economic bleeding would strengthen our moral fiber and lead to the next boom. In his memoirs, Herbert Hoover attributed this harsh philosophy to Andrew Mellon, his wealthy treasury secretary. Hoover described Mellon and his followers as "leave it alone liquidationists" who "felt that government must keep its hands off and let the slump liquidate itself." Wrote Hoover:

> Mr. Mellon had only one formula: "Liquidate labor, liquidate stocks, liquidate the farmers, liquidate real estate." He insisted that, when the people get an inflation brainstorm, the only way to get it out of their blood is to let it collapse. He held that even a panic was not altogether a bad thing. He said: "It will purge the rottenness out of the system. High costs of living and high living will come down. People will work harder, live a more moral life. Values will be adjusted, and enterprising people will pick up the wrecks from less competent people. . . ."[2]

It's not at all clear if Mellon actually said these things. Either way, Hoover's account provides an apt description of Social Darwinism at its cruelest.

During the 1920s, no one worried very much about an economic depression. America, now the world's largest creditor nation, seemed to have found the key to permanent prosperity. It was fueled by mass consumerism, rising productivity, thousands of new inventions, scientific management, and abundant natural and human resources. Rising debt seemed like a blessing rather than a curse. The "consumer" was invented during this period—

and so was the installment plan. It is estimated that by 1926, "65 percent of motorcars were purchased on installment credit. Department stores sold over 40 percent of goods on credit."[3] In the Roaring Twenties buying on margin became endemic. As stocks rose, you could borrow against them to buy more stocks, which in turn pushed the stock prices up even higher. Serious scholars during those years marveled at the boom and more than a few felt it would never end—that capitalism had finally escaped the boom-bust cycle.[4]

In the buildup to the crash, we can spot the usual suspects: easy credit, market manipulation, few regulatory safeguards, and a large dose of herd euphoria. But people felt confident anyway. For one thing, they thought the Federal Reserve, formed in 1913, would prevent a serious panic by adjusting the money supply, supervising the banking community, and halting bank runs.

People were not prepared for the financial bust—much less the utter devastation that followed in the "real" economy. To many it looked as though Karl Marx's prediction of capitalism's demise had finally come true. Not only did the stock market lose approximately 90 percent of its value in the space of two years, but the gross national product declined by half and more than a quarter of the nonagricultural workforce lost jobs. No economic system could endure such devastation for long. And no sensible nation would allow such a crisis to ever happen again.

The shock of the Depression led to a new "common sense" understanding among most academics and policy makers, as well as the public: The government had to regulate, and regulate heavily, to keep the economy from running amok. John Maynard Keynes, arguably the era's leading economic theorist, provided the lens through which most of post-Depression America viewed financial markets: "Speculators may do no harm as bubbles on a steady stream of enterprise. But the position is serious when enterprise becomes a bubble on a whirlpool of speculation. When the capital development of a country becomes a by-product of the activities of a casino, the job is likely to be ill done."[5]

Andrew Mellon's "liquidationist," anti-regulation, social Darwinian, laissez-faire ideology was dead. The New Deal era consensus was that finance needed intensive regulation or it would destroy itself, taking the rest of us with it. The government created a slew of agencies and programs to protect us all from fantasy finance. The Securities and Exchange Commission regulated the stock market. The Federal Deposit Insurance Corporation protected individual bank accounts against bank runs and failures.[6] The Glass-Steagall Act of 1933 erected a firewall between investment banking and commercial banking to protect businesses and consumers from financial speculation and manipulation. The Federal Housing Administration enabled people with modest incomes to buy their own homes. And for the first time, bankruptcy laws were extended to average wage earners.

During the Depression, the financial "cauldron of innovation" came not from the free-market casino but from the government. Take the financial instrument called the mortgage. It had been kicking around since the twelfth century. English common law held that anyone who loaned money to you for a property had a claim on that property if you did not repay the loan. By the turn of the twentieth century in the New World, the terms of private-sector mortgages were exceedingly stringent. To get a home mortgage, you usually had to come up with a 50 percent down payment as well as interest payments over the next five years. At the end of the five years the loan balance came due in full, often forcing the borrower to find yet another five-year loan. As a result, home ownership was limited to those with means. So for nine hundred years, private financial markets were unable to reap the profits of mass home financing.

The housing market collapsed entirely during the Depression. The New Deal forcefully resurrected it by creating the long-term, fixed-rate, self-amortizing mortgage, and guaranteeing the loans of buyers who met certain guidelines. The New Deal's Home Owners' Loan Corporation introduced the fifteen-year mortgage. The Federal Housing Administration then offered twenty-year terms. In the 1950s, the standard term increased to thirty years. Home ownership was finally within the grasp of the general population. And the government, not the private sector, had invented the financial instrument that made it all possible. (Sneak preview: When the private sector finally gets back to applying its creativity to the mortgage market, all hell breaks loose.)

The Depression so frightened America from top to bottom that most people welcomed the heavy hand of government to protect the economy from even deeper collapse. The government's draconian economic controls during World War II further legitimized strong federal supervision. It seemed that the power of financial markets was forever tamed.

Over time, however, the fast developing world economy would undercut the New Deal regulatory regime. It would take about fifty years, but the power of money-making-money prevailed. Eventually, the casino reopened.

Currency exchange rates were both the symbol of strict financial controls after World War II and the key battlefield. The allied leaders who gathered in Bretton Woods, New Hampshire, in July 1944 understood that the new postwar system would only work if global capital flows were tightly controlled. They feared currency speculation,[7] which they'd seen plenty of during the Depression. They recognized that allowing corporations, investors, and speculators to zing money from country to country to game the currencies was destabilizing. So they set the value of global currencies in dollars, pegged the dollar to gold at $35 an ounce, and instituted strict capital controls from country to country.

This system held together until 1970 or so. But then fixed exchange rates began to present a problem. Europe and Japan were rebuilding rapidly, fueling a rise in trade and renewed world competition. The cost of containing communism kept climbing, and wars were breaking out all over. The United States pumped out billions of dollars for operations in Vietnam and around the globe. By 1971, the world was awash with dollars. Inflation was mounting and a run on U.S. gold seemed imminent.[8]

In response to all this, President Richard Nixon instituted World War II–like wage and price controls to constrain inflation. He also freed the dollar from the gold standard. The Bretton Woods era was over. The international arena was opened again to fast-moving funds, and once again speculators had plenty of room to maneuver.

But the memory of the Depression was still strong, and many New Deal regulations and attitudes held, constraining the U.S. financial sector. Meanwhile, the sixties revolt against authority was sowing new doubts about the private sector. In the movie *The Graduate*, the businessman whom Dustin Hoffman was cuckolding had one word to say to him: "plastics." The audience got the joke—modern corporate life was artificial and consumer life was shallow and trite. Like plastic, corporations had no soul. The cultural climate was not conducive to the financial casino.

Enter Milton Friedman. It would be an exaggeration to say that the University of Chicago economist single-handedly undermined New Deal ideology and repelled the New Left's assault on consumerism. But he certainly led the way.

With war raging and the environment under siege, many people, young and old, thought that corporations needed to become more "socially responsible." Friedman was appalled, especially when he saw some corporate leaders succumbing to such ideas. Friedman believed that capitalism was the best and only protection for individual freedoms—and yet it seemed to him that no one was willing to stand up for it. (He so detested government interference in the economy that he even opposed the existence of the Food and Drug Administration.) In a widely read *New York Times Magazine* article published on September 13, 1970, Friedman rejected "the present climate of opinion, with its widespread aversion to 'capitalism,' 'profits,' the 'soulless corporation.'"

Like Adam Smith, Friedman argued that capitalism worked best when each person and enterprise was free to pursue maximum profit. Any additional economic goals, he said, would be foolish and dangerous. Pursuing profit made markets efficient, and through the invisible hand, enabled society to prosper. Furthermore, these profit-making pursuits protected society from "the iron fist of government bureaucrats." Freedom and economic necessity demanded that the government stay out of the economy. As Friedman put it: "There is one and only one social responsibility of business—to use its resources and engage in activities designed to increase its profits so long as it stays within the rules of the game, which is to say, engages in open and free competition without deception or fraud."[9]

But Friedman had his sights set on more than just the New Left and its semi-socialistic ideologies. He saw the entire New Deal as perilous to both the free market and individual freedom. He knew that to defeat the intrusive regulatory regime, he had to undermine the prevailing common sense about the causes of the Great Depression. People would continue to cling to New Deal controls if they thought that abandoning them would cause another crash.

Friedman tried to refute the whole idea that the Great Depression was caused by fundamental flaws of capitalism—the same flaws predicted by Marx and other leftist economic scholars. Many economists, even nonsocialists like Keynes, thought the Depression proved that capitalism was prone to cataclysmic cyclical crises. The crises were due to overproduction of goods that couldn't be sold, or to the underconsumption of goods that workers couldn't afford when their wages were depressed, or to the inherent instability within financial markets. This view of capitalism had led to reforms that, in Friedman's mind, shackled the capitalist spirit, hampered free markets, and threatened individual freedoms.

Friedman and coauthor Anna Schwartz argued in their ground-breaking book, *A Monetary History of the United States, 1867–1960*, that the economy collapsed in the 1930s not because of systemic faults, but rather because of human error: the Federal Reserve's poor management of the money supply. The problem was not the "internal contradictions of capitalism," but rather the Fed's tight money policies during and after the stock market boom.

Current Fed chairman Ben Bernanke fully supports this line of reasoning. As he put it in 2002,

> The correct interpretation of the 1920s, then, is not the popular one—that the stock market got overvalued, crashed, and caused a Great Depression. The true story is that monetary policy tried overzealously to stop the rise in stock prices. But the main effect of the tight monetary policy, as Benjamin Strong had predicted, was to slow the economy—both domestically and, through the workings of the gold standard, abroad. The slowing economy, together with rising interest rates, was in turn a major factor in precipitating the stock market crash.[10]

Friedman's revisionism was music to the ears of 1980s conservatives like Ronald Reagan and British prime minister Margaret Thatcher. During his administration (1980–88), Reagan proceeded to "unleash" the private sector, dismantling all manner of New Deal controls, and crippling labor unions along the way.

The Reaganites also reorganized the tax structure to allow more wealth to accumulate at the top. Under the newly minted theory of the "Laffer Curve," tax cuts would spur economic growth, which would increase federal revenue rather than deplete it. Prosperity would trickle up, down, and around for all. If the tax cuts caused a short-term jump in government debt, so be it. That would provide fiscal pressure to eliminate New Deal and Great Society programs that reduced the incentive to work and shackled free markets.

A remarkable statistic from the Reagan years shows just how well the tax cuts transferred wealth to the superrich. From 1983 to 1989, the top 0.5 percent of all families saw their combined wealth increase by $1.45 trillion, while the wealth of the bottom 40 percent of families went down by $256 billion. Remarkably, during those same years the federal debt rose by $1.49 trillion.[11] It was as if the entire federal debt had been awarded directly to the superrich. The financial casino now had the capital it needed to spin the wheel—as well as the freedom from regulation.

In fact, conditions were absolutely ripe for a new era of fantasy finance. Astute traders realized that all the new wealth that the rich had poured into the market needed to be deployed. Those who could offer high returns to the wealthy could themselves become fabulously wealthy.

As the Reagan administration eased antitrust regulations, leveraged mergers and acquisitions (buying up companies with borrowed money) became the rage. Companies were chopped up, shut down, and auctioned away, and investors took home the loot. People still argue about whether these mergers and acquisitions helped to modernize the American economy or undermine it. Certainly they hastened the decline of manufacturing in this country. Very often the buyouts were unproductive. There are shelves of books describing in graphic detail the pillaging of the industrial landscape, the junk bond high jinks of Michael Milken, and the indictments that rained down on some of the players. It's now clear that all that was just a sideshow to the main entertainment of fantasy finance.

———

President Reagan opened a new, lucrative casino when he deregulated savings and loans banks. The New Deal had clamped fairly strict regulations on what savings banks could and could not do. They were supposed to take in savings and give out home mortgages. The interest rates they could pay on deposits had a ceiling. Tight regulations governed how much of their money they could lend to commercial enterprises and more risky investments.

In the 1980s, pressure from the banking community, the changing economic landscape, and the prevailing antiregulatory ideology enabled Reagan administration officials to drop many of these restrictions. Now these thrift institutions could attract more funds by offering higher interest rates and make far riskier loans, especially in the booming commercial real estate market.

Before we get too far into the story, we need to meet another troublesome financial innovation: "moral hazard," a term borrowed from the insurance industry. If I have full insurance on my bicycle, I might not lock it up properly since it's not such a big deal (to me) if it's stolen—the insurance company will replace it. So, at least in theory, more insurance could lead to lazier bicycle riders—a moral hazard—who enable more bicycle thefts. In finance, the bicycle is risk. If I know I will be bailed out if I assume risk and fail, I'll assume more and more risk and let you bail me out if I fail.[12] Free-market conservatives use this to argue that we should let enterprises fail even if it causes short-term pain for society as a whole. They believe that after a relatively short period of time, the economy will right itself and be stronger than ever. And most importantly, the gamblers will not have been rewarded and the moral hazard is dampened as we move forward. (When we're talking about one or two banks at a time, that makes sense. When we're talking about the entire financial industry as a whole, it could take a decade and a world war to end a depression as it did in the 1930s.)

Here's the connection to the savings and loan banks (S&Ls). In addition to regulations on savings-bank practices, the New Deal also protected the millions of Americans who put their money in savings banks. The banks were required to follow prudent lending rules. At the same time, savings accounts of up to a certain amount were insured by the FDIC. For decades, savings and loans provided modest but secure returns for savers, and made secure housing loans that helped fuel the postwar housing boom.

The deregulations under Reagan allowed the S&Ls to offer higher interest rates and make more speculative loans and investments. However, even the free-market ideologues knew better than to eliminate the FDIC guarantees on savings. That could lead to depositor losses, bank runs, and financial panic. Instead the Reaganites got the FDIC to *increase* the level of deposit it would insure, further increasing the appeal of the S&Ls. Entrepreneurs immediately recognized that savings banks could become private money machines with very little downside. You could start or take over a bank, attract lots of customers with your higher interest rates, dramatically expand the balance sheet with risky investments, spend lavishly on yourself, and yet be able to tell customers that their money was safe and sound, FDIC insured. It was a whopper of a free-market moral hazard.

With the upside interest-rate regulations lifted, a host of casino players got into the business, opening up savings banks, enticing depositors with very attractive rates, and then placing bets on commercial development projects all over the country. Along the way they used the bank's money like a private piggy bank, buying planes, art, condos, and other personal booty. During the mid-1980s, U.S. savings banks were the best financial casino on the globe.

Then they went bust—in predictable ways. As savings and loan money flooded into commercial real estate, a construction boom led to overproduction of shopping centers and office complexes. Eventually the supply outstripped the demand. The bubble burst, leading to the collapse of more than one thousand savings and loan institutions. The government had a mess on its hands.

When the thousand or so banks failed, a few looters got nabbed, but most of the wily entrepreneurs walked away unharmed and vastly richer. The government took over the banks and their devalued assets, and protected the individual deposits as promised. Over the next decade the government sold off the assets. Taxpayers footed the $200 billion bill. Moral hazards always come at a price.

You'd think the S&L crisis would have given pause to the deregulatory orthodoxy. Not a chance. By the end of the Reagan era the casino was still wide open for business.

Looking back, you can see how the savings-and-loan moral hazard would lead eventually to bigger and bigger bailouts. The principle was now firmly established: We can't afford to let the system collapse even if it means bailing out thousands of venal, greedy entrepreneurs who have gambled their venture into the ground, grabbing riches along the way. We must bail out even the reckless, because it protects the innocent as well.

As the financial sector grew, the serious players knew that the government wouldn't let them fail—even if key investors and traders were not specifically covered by government insurance or regulations. Moral hazard was built into the system. Individual banks and financial companies might fail, but to protect all of us from a systemic meltdown, the feds would have to come to the rescue. The combination of deregulatory ideology and moral hazard was hypocritical: If you're a winner, it's a free market. If you lose big, we bail you out. Who wouldn't bet heavy in that kind of casino?

By the end of the Reagan years, vast pools of wealth were forming as astute investment managers generated enormous returns of 25, 30, 40 percent or more, year after year. Hedge funds, which had been minor players since they emerged in the 1950s, became much more popular with millionaire investors like George Soros and grew in influence. (Pension funds and college endowments would also become heavy investors in these unregulated funds.)

During the New Deal such outlandish returns would have been held suspect and investigated. But in the new deregulatory era there was a far greater acceptance, even admiration, for the fast-growing financial investments of the superrich. Wouldn't we all have liked to get a piece of that casino action?

Our government financial watchdogs argued that the government had no business regulating these funds because they were only for the rich and for large institutional investors—the general public was not at risk. If the rich and institutional investors wanted to play in this high stakes casino that was their right. More than that, the idea was that government regulation would get in the way of the market-based regulation investors would impose on their own. Or as Alan Greenspan put it, "Indeed, institutional investors have accounted for a growing share of hedge fund investments, and they can and should protect their own interests rather than rely on the limited regulatory protections. . . ."[13]

With so much wealth sloshing around at the top, it was only a matter of time before clever financial traders developed new money-making-money products that promised ever higher returns. And with deregulation in full throttle there were few pesky government officials around with the time or inclination to question the soundness of those instruments, or the systemic risks they created.

Welcome to the brave new world of derivatives.

five

The Oracle Blesses Derivatives, the Newest Game in the Casino

DERIVATIVES. Now there's a word that opens our sweat glands. Some of us last faced derivatives in calculus and ran for cover. But here we are again, grappling with a type of financial instrument that is supposedly so hard to understand that no one should attempt the feat, certainly not policy makers. Better we should leave it to the really smart people in the financial sector. Let the quantitative experts, the "quants", hold the high ground. Let the sophisticated traders create the derivatives and profit from them. And the rest of us? Duck and cover. (Or if you live in the Milwaukee area, put your hand on your wallet, because derivatives were what the school systems bought without knowing it.)

Sorry, but we're going to have to give it a try. It's the only way we can reclaim our citizenship (and our tax dollars) from the masters of high finance. For it is with derivatives that the toxic waste really got its start, back in the late 1980s and early 1990s. That was when the financiers finally got their hands on computers and figured out how to make complexity pay off.

So let's hang in there. I'm betting you and I can do this. We surely can't do worse than the policy makers who, back then, totally abdicated their regulatory responsibilities and put our entire economy at risk—despite the clearest warnings.

One clear warning came on May 19, 1994, when James L. Bothwell, on behalf of the General Accounting Office (the GAO, now the Government Accountability Office) testified before Congress. His words were chilling because they so directly warned of the colossal meltdown that hit us in 2008.

He began by defining derivatives as part innovation and part casino: "Among their benefits, derivatives provide end-users with opportunities to better manage financial risks associated with their business transactions, called hedging. They also provide opportunities to profit from anticipated movements in market prices or rates, called speculating."[1]

This spanking new casino, Mr. Bothwell pointed out, was not just a few slots at a dusty Nevada gas station. No, by 1994, the derivatives casino had about $12.1 trillion whizzing around the globe. And the business was heavily concentrated. As of December 1992, Bothwell said, "the top seven domestic bank OTC [unregulated "over the counter"] derivatives dealers accounted for more than 90 percent of total U.S. bank derivatives activity."[2] (The "top seven" were major investment banks and commercial banks. Within those institutions derivative groups are composed of traders, salespeople, and statisticians, who create, trade, and sell derivatives.)

Bothwell neglects to mention that the casino was already gushing profits (and bonuses) for the investment bankers who packaged, sold, and traded derivatives. I have yet to find a good estimate of the amount "earned" from that $12.1 trillion, but let's assume it's at least half of 1 percent. That would bring the house cut from the casino to around $60 billion—and that was back in 1994, when the dealers were just getting started.

So let's recap. We have some kind of derivative financial instruments, not yet described, that do things that add up to the trillions of dollars. We know there are relatively few players moving them around. We also know that these instruments are good when they hedge risk and not so good when they enhance speculation—that is, betting.

Why should we worry about speculation? Bothwell pointed out that because the trading and use of derivatives is so concentrated and the links between those who create, buy, and trade them are so tight, a "sudden failure or abrupt withdrawal from trading of any of these large U.S. dealers could cause liquidity problems in the markets and could also pose risks to others including federally insured banks and the financial system as a whole."[3]

Translation? Bothwell was warning us that derivatives involved big, big trades and big, big bets on things like whether interest rates go up or down, or whether certain currencies change value. If a large derivatives trader lost big on its bets, the company might go bust. And if it defaulted, the cash this market needed to operate (liquidity) might dry up, causing others to fold up as well. Bothwell was also cautioning that the market for derivatives was so big that even federally insured banks (which had been loaning money to derivatives dealers) would suffer horribly if a major trader went belly-up. In short, he's describing the systemic risk of a market that is so large and incestuous that it would not easily withstand failure by a major player. He was warning that if a derivatives domino fell, it might knock down the banking and credit system dominoes as well.

Bothwell predicted that if one of the big derivative traders did collapse, the feds probably wouldn't intervene right away, since derivative trading was unregulated. But if insured banks got hit, the government would have to jump in—putting taxpayers on the hook:

> Although the federal government would not necessarily intervene just to keep a major OTC derivatives dealer from failing, the federal government would be likely to intervene to keep the financial system functioning in cases of severe financial stress. While federal regulators have often been able to keep financial disruptions from becoming crises, in some cases intervention has and could result in a financial bailout paid for by taxpayers.[4]

Sound eerily familiar?

So what was Bothwell seeking with his alarming testimony back in 1994? He wanted a modicum of regulation. He didn't trust the industry's claim that it was policing itself. He wanted new accounting standards that clarified the risks he knew the traders were hiding. He wanted oversight of over-the-counter trades. He wanted to be sure that the insurance industry, which was then getting into the derivatives act, didn't get burned. In short, he wanted a reasonably regulated casino.

But Bothwell, like virtually every policy maker, genuflected before the financial god of "innovation." Major investment banks, the big players on the Street, had surely warned him that if the government imposed regulations they didn't like, they would move the business to London or Paris. So on his knees Bothwell recites the catechism:

> We believe that innovation and creativity are the strengths of the U.S. financial services industry and that these strengths should not be eroded or forced outside the United States by excessive regulation. . . . The issue is one of striking a proper balance between (1) allowing the U.S. financial services industry to grow and innovate and (2) protecting the safety and soundness of the nation's financial system.[5]

What a reasonable guy. Derivatives, he was saying, seem to be very useful and profitable and innovative, and lots of institutions have put a great deal of money into them. But they also seem to be risky. So as a prudent protector of the commonweal, the Congress should bring some order to this market of newfangled financial widgets. And this was in 1994!

But Bothwell's calls for caution were drowned out by none other than "the Oracle," Dr. Alan Greenspan, chairman of the Federal Reserve.[6] Recall that by 1994, the economy, employment levels, and incomes were heading up. Greenspan, President Clinton, and later Clinton's treasury secretary, Robert Rubin, were more or less on the same page. Greenspan was a very smart and experienced economist who projected an aura of knowing every nook and cranny of the financial system. So when he said,

"Hands off!" people listened, especially members of Congress who definitely didn't know much about these new derivatives. Of course Congress was also getting an earful from lobbyists for the big time Wall Street derivative players. The lobbyists even started a public relations campaign to expunge the word "derivatives" from the press: They preferred "securities."[7] Here's how Greenspan put the case against derivative regulations in March 1995:

> Markets function most efficiently when both parties to financial transactions are free to enter into transactions at their own discretion, unhampered by any perceived need to serve the interests of their counterparties. To date, losses in the financial markets have not led to broader systemic problems. Moreover, both dealers and their customers, somewhat shaken by the volatility of recent markets, are responding to these events by exercising greater caution. If discipline from incurring losses from mistakes were mitigated, vigilance would be relaxed, the market's natural adaptive response would be blunted, and the value of decentralized market decisions as allocators of scarce capital resources would be reduced. I believe that we should start with the principle that parties to financial transactions are responsible for their own decisions and only use regulation to adjust the balance of responsibilities between the parties cautiously after the benefit has been clearly established.[8]

What is the Oracle really saying?

1. Markets by definition are efficient. They are by far the best way to determine utility and value and to allocate scarce resources.
2. If a product, financial or otherwise, sucks, it will disappear from the market as fast as the Edsel.

3. Since there is a very large and vibrant market for financial derivatives, by definition, they must be good—until
the market decides they are not.

4. The market is the best regulator of derivatives, and regulators should stay away.

5. Besides, if you do try to regulate the derivative innovators, who obviously are much brighter than you'll ever
be, they will outsmart you by finding new ways around
your dumb rules. So don't waste your time, their time, or
my time.

Nevertheless, Congress did consider mandating new accounting rules to accommodate derivatives. As it was, derivative transactions didn't even appear on the books. Banks and investment
houses argued that it would be almost impossible to include
derivatives in their accounting. They would be really, really hard
to price because they were so volatile. They would make your
company's books gyrate and give a foggy, inaccurate picture to
investors. Wouldn't it be best to just keep that trillion dollars
of risk and hedging off the books, out of sight and far away from
both investors and regulators? Oracle Greenspan put it simply
when testifying in 1995: "It would be a serious mistake to respond
to these developments by singling out the derivative instruments
for special regulatory treatment. Such a response would create
artificial incentives to structure transactions on the basis of regulatory rules rather than on the economic characteristics of the
transactions themselves."[9]

The Oracle prevailed.

————————

It's downright amusing to watch the GAO and Greenspan
wriggle their way out of even mentioning the distended profits
generated by derivative trading. Greenspan, of course, believes
that it is none of the government's business. The free market is
supposed to create billionaires. They are the smart and deserving

risk takers. (There's a reason why he loves Ayn Rand, the author who stressed individualism and limited government in books such as *The Virtue of Selfishness*.) Derivative traders deserve what the market will bear. If they are overpaid the market will move funds away from them. There is no such thing as lavish profits. That's the miracle of the market.

Reality is somewhat less miraculous. We will soon discover there's an unfortunate connection between the get-rich derivatives industry and the current financial crash.

So what *are* these golden derivatives? Unfortunately the official definition uses the word we are trying to define: They are the broad class of financial instruments that *derive* their value based on the value or movement of other financial indicators, prices, or instruments.[10] Clear as mud?

If you play in a fantasy sports league you should have an intuitive grasp of derivatives. A fantasy baseball team, for example, is composed of the statistics that are derived from real major league baseball players. You "own" a team much the same way someone owns a derivative. What gives it value is that you're involved in a bet with other fantasy baseball "owners" in your league to see which of your derivative teams accumulates the best statistics. In effect, you are speculating on the stats derived from real major-league players, but those players don't know they are playing on your team. You own only the derivative stats, not the real thing.

Let's consider a few financial examples. You could buy a derivative that is connected to whether interest rates rise or fall, or on which way exchange rates are going to move. Or instead of buying the underlying stocks that make up the Dow Jones Industrial Average you could buy a DJIA derivative that gains or loses value based only on how the Dow Jones Industrial Average moves. You could have a derivative that goes up or down with the price of oil, or just the price of oil in Japan or even the difference in oil prices between Texas and Norway. There are countless varieties of derivatives that allow you to swap income flows. A bank derivative group can design for you a derivative with another party so that you give up adjustable-rate income in exchange for fixed-rate income. Or you can give up interest income in dollars for interest income in euros. In short, because derivatives don't actually have to contain a "real" item (like a stock, a bond, or a barrel of oil) there is no limit to the kinds of derivatives your banker can (and does) create. What's more, as we now know, most of these transactions take place off the books of your firm and are unregulated. No wonder the GAO sounded the alarm.

But why would anyone want these devices? The answer is risk. Derivatives are created for people who want to get rid of risk by dumping it onto someone else, or who want to speculate by picking up the risk. When people buy derivatives they are accepting someone else's risk at a price that makes it worthwhile. Capitalist ideologues love to brag about how our system consists of millions of risk takers pushing the envelope of innovation. We're a country of swashbuckling entrepreneurs putting our life, limb, and hard-earned cash on the line for dreams that others didn't have the guts to believe in. Well, not quite. Our entrepreneurs also want to hedge every risk they can, in every way they can. And if they do take risks, they prefer, as Satyajit Das put it in *Traders, Guns and Money*, to "play with other people's money." The derivative traders—that is the ten or so big financial houses that run this show—cater to this endemic, risk-averse desire and earn a pretty penny doing so. Yes, entrepreneurs take risks but they're not stupid. If they can hedge their bets at a reasonable price, they will.

The classic example used repeatedly by the GAO in its discussion of derivatives is the industrious U.S. importer of an expensive piece of highly engineered German machinery due for delivery in a year. Unfortunately the price is in marks (these were pre-euro days)—let's say 10 million marks. You, the American importer, will have to pay for the machine in marks one year down the road when it is delivered. While the price in dollars may be a good one today, it might not be if the mark goes up in value compared to the dollar over the next year. This could be quite a price hike, and it might just bust your business. So what do you do? In the 1990s you called your friendly Bankers Trust representative, and he'd design a derivative that would allow you to pay a slight premium for the right to have access to 10 million marks a year from now—at today's exchange rate. More likely your derivatives salesperson already spotted this problem and called you with such a product. You jump at the chance. Your banker makes a fee by selling you the instrument. He may also make a fee on selling the swap to another party that allows the banker to hedge your interest-rate risk. Or the bank may repackage the whole thing and sell it to someone else. You don't care. You've got your exchange rate for the 10 million marks locked in. That's the wholesome side of derivatives—protecting your firm's risk. Also, the collective shifting or risk through many such trades may be socially useful as well, since, when it works, risk is moving toward those who can better handle it.

But sometimes your friendly derivatives banker might try to sell you stuff you don't need, but that is very profitable to him and his bank. Satyajit Das's highly entertaining book on derivatives is framed by a set of such deals involving the managers of an Indonesian noodle firm. The noodle company's American banker noticed that the company might benefit if it hedged loans it had made in the Indonesian currency with a swap using dollar-denominated loans—a custom-made derivative the bank could create for the noodle company. So far so good, because the interest rate loan in the local currency was much higher than was the interest rate on dollar-denominated loans. After a while the banker reported that the derivative actually went up in value. Would they like to sell it and book the profit, which was several hundred thousand dollars? Of course. They sold, they profited, and then they bought from their banker a more complicated derivative that was virtually impossible to understand. It involved a bigger bet, which in turn led to another bet. The noodle makers had been lured into the casino and were playing with the high rollers—except they didn't know the game. One of their biggest bets would only work if interest rates didn't fluctuate very much. Unfortunately, they did. And the noodlemakers soon lost over $400 million!

In effect the banker was like a pusher. He got the noodlers hooked on making some fast money through currency speculation. At first they did (although it turned out the banker had made even more than they did on that deal, which they had no way of figuring out at the time). Meanwhile, every transaction generated more fees for the bank and bonus money for the banker. The more complex the instrument sold, the more fees embedded in it. A veteran banker friend of Satyarjit Das put it this way as he was training new derivative salespeople: "Sonny, give the guy a win first up. A nibble. He'll be hooked. Then, you reel him in real slow. That's how you land the big ones."[11]

Das provides example after example of unscrupulous bank salespeople and traders who preyed upon companies, hooking them into complex products they didn't need or understand. The stories show how easy it is to slide from legitimate hedging activities into the casino. When the casino is working for you, you look like a genius. But sooner or later you're going to lose because you have no idea what you're doing. Meanwhile the derivative pros are making money from you on your way up and on your way down.

But let's be clear. This is not about good or bad people. The noodle makers waltzed into the fantasy-finance casino because they were as greedy as the bankers. Instead, our focus should be on the casino and the derivative gaming tables that can and did crash the economy.

Next comes a story that should be required reading for every public financial official and every firm that is trying to push financial instruments onto public agencies—starting in Wisconsin. It is the case of Orange County and Robert Citron, its treasurer, back in the late 1980s. Citron, who had no financial background, found his way onto the board of supervisors for Orange County, California, an affluent area north of San Diego. The county had considerable funds, and its internal investment rules were very conservative. It wanted its money safely invested in short-term maturities that wouldn't go bust.

But Citron was a sitting duck for derivatives traders, who showed him how he could more or less conform to the county's rules, yet get much better returns. At the time, interest rates were dropping. The derivatives salespeople showered Citron with "securities" that provided better returns than any other county or state was getting on their cash. All he had to do was buy these complex derivatives, which supposedly were based upon very secure federal bonds and such. (You can hear the same refrain on the Wisconsin school board tapes.)

Citron heeded the siren's call, and for a while he looked like a hero. Orange County "earned" better returns than any other public entity around. To maintain his star status, all he had to do was continue to follow the lead of his derivative pushers. And push they did. They piled "innovative" instruments, one on top of the other until they were stacked like planes at JFK. They used his safe government investments as collateral to "leverage" bigger and bigger bets. In effect, Citron put up the county's money to borrow lots more, which was then bet on riskier and riskier plays. He also was the mark of all marks for the derivative houses, which saw the Orange County deal as a big bucks operation. As Das put it:

> Every banker and trader prostrated themselves before him to get a share of the business. There was just so much money to be made. The dealers made money on the notes they sold to Orange County, they made money on the derivatives they used to hedge the structures, they made money on the money they lent Orange County so they could do the same all over again. It was a proverbial money tree.[12]

Best of all, the bankers risked none of their own money. They used Orange County funds on the cheap to make their plays. It was as if Citron was staking the bankers to play alongside him at the casino tables. As Das writes, the bankers "got cheap money but took no risk as they made sure that all their bets were fully hedged. Who was paying for the party? It turned out to be Orange County taxpayers."[13]

During their hot run, Citron was earning returns twice what other counties could achieve. He was *the* man of public finance. When another derivative dealer who didn't get in on the action questioned the soundness of some of his investments, Citron slapped him down: "You don't understand the type of investment strategies that we are using. I would suggest that you not seek doing business with Orange County."[14]

But lady luck can leave you in a hurry when you're placing bigger and bigger bets that you really don't understand. By 1994 Citron had a mountain of chips on the table. He had $7 billion in county funds, which the bankers had leveraged, with loans, up to about $20 billion. Even Citron's bankers started to worry that they should go easy on this guy for fear they could jeopardize all the profits they were milking. But they didn't slow the game down. Things went smoothly as long as interest rates stayed low.

Citron looked in the mirror and saw one really smart dude. When asked why he thought interest rates would continue to stay low, he replied "I am one of the largest investors in America. I know these things."[15] (In fact he may not have been playing with a full deck. He later said that he had made some of his most brilliant investment decisions using a mail order astrologer's chart.[16])

The casino party ended with a bang when Greenspan pushed interest rates up sharply in 1994. Citron lost all of his chips almost overnight. Not only did his portfolio show $1.5 billion in losses, but the county had to come up with more cash in a hurry for collateral needed to secure their many leveraged positions. It was a mess. The county filed for bankruptcy on December 6, 1994. The poor suffered drastic cuts in services as at least sixteen hundred county workers lost their jobs.[17]

As it turned out, many other counties also had been lured into the derivative casino by their profit-hungry bankers. Dozens of guardians of public-sector funds couldn't resist the promise of higher and higher returns, and many lost the public's money along the way. The dealers got their hands slapped and several had to make restitution of sorts. Still, the major derivative banks, brokerages, and investment houses walked away with vast sums. When it comes to profits and bonuses, what happens in the derivative casino, stays in the derivative casino.

———

Let's keep following the money. The case of Orange County, like that of the Indonesian noodle company, shows how easy it was for astute bankers to use opaque financial instruments to lure their marks into risky investments. These examples and many others like them (Procter & Gamble, Gibson Greeting Cards, etc.) also reveal the mismatch between the sophisticated derivative pusher and the marks who so obviously were in over their heads.

The collapse of Long-Term Capital Management, however, demonstrated that even the most sophisticated hedge fund managers could also lose at the casino and in doing so threaten the entire financial system. In fact, bigger and smarter meant even more danger. (We're still in the 1990s. You'd be right to wonder why we didn't learn more from these events.)

John Meriwether, the guru of derivatives traders, set up LTCM, which many heralded as the gold standard of hedge funds. By this point the term "hedge fund" had lost its original meaning. You did not put money into a hedge fund to hedge your bets, as was the case with the first such investment funds during the 1950s. Instead, you put money in these funds to play the casino, shoulder to shoulder with the hedge fund's creators—playing alongside the smart money. To play with Meriwether you had to be very rich: You couldn't join his hedge fund unless you anted up $10 million. Here's what you got. For the privilege of playing with a master casino guru, Meriwether charged 2 percent of the money you gave him plus 25 percent of the winnings. By 1994, he had gathered a $1.5-billion stake from his investors. His 2 percent up front was a cool $30 million.

Starting with a fat wad, Meriwether rounded up the best and the brightest traders, including a dozen or so Ph.D.s, and two of his former finance professors. They were certain they could bend the casino odds again and again. And they had all the cash they needed: Major investment banks loaned them billions, often without requiring any collateral. After a few years the value of their fund grew to about $4.7 billion. They leveraged that into another $125 billion with borrowed money. Then they used derivatives to place bets that totaled $1.25 trillion. That's quite a pile of chips (more than a million piles with each pile containing a million chips!).

At first, Meriwether and company played it safe, looking for slight differences in prices among similar items in different markets. They knew the same items ought to end up at the same price sooner or later, so they bet on the cheaper one and sold their bet on the more expensive one until the prices matched up. That's called arbitrage.[18] When you placed billions on such bets you could make real money. While 1994 was a terrible year for Wall Street as a whole, Meriwether made a 28 percent return on the fund's initial equity. Let's pause and do the math. Twenty-eight percent of $1.5 billion comes to $420 million—a nice return for the fund as whole. Meriwether and his partners took 25 percent, for a total of $105 million. Not bad.

It got better. In 1995 they got lucky with interest-rate plays. The Kobe earthquake in Japan increased market volatility and, by chance, dramatically increased the value of certain options they had bet upon. That year they "earned" a 59 percent return. In 1996 they started winning bets with other nations, almost sure bets, because of close relationships they had developed with central banks overseas. That year they returned 44 percent on their capital. Just imagine how smart and lucky you would feel with returns of 28 percent, 59 percent, and 44 percent back to back to back.

Economic theory tells us that competition should have driven returns back toward the national average as more firms entered into this lucrative business. In fact by 1997, Meriwether's firm did start to feel the heat. It was becoming harder and harder to find those special bets at the casino, because many new hedge funds were crowding the table. As a result, in 1997 the fund's returns dropped to "only" 17 percent.

As they built up their wad of surplus capital, it became harder and harder to properly invest it. Frank Partnoy in *Infectious Greed* writes that in 1998 Meriwether and his partners "agreed that they would reduce the size of the fund by about $3 billion, because of concern that they might not be able to find enough good investments. . . ."[19] Capitalism was doing its thing. High profits had attracted more players, and the space to secure superprofits had narrowed.

But Long-Term Capital Management was sure they had the best talent. They also were sure they had prepared for the worst. They had placed a lot of bets on a whole bunch of different casino tables and they thought they had hedged themselves pretty well. They also figured that these tables were far enough apart so that there was no way that all their bets could turn against them at the same time. In technical terms, they thought their investments were not "correlated." As Partnoy put it, "They had believed their portfolios were sufficiently diversified to survive even if the ball on the roulette wheel landed on black several times in a row."[20]

However, 1997–98 saw turmoil. Many hedge funds had placed bets in emerging markets in developing nations, expecting good things. Then Russia defaulted on its debts. Banks that were making big loans to hedge funds wanted more collateral. Hedge funds had to sell assets to come up with that collateral—which drove down asset prices. The rout was on. As Partnoy says, "all of LTCM's supposedly uncorrelated bets were going down, at the same time. The ball was landing on black, over and over again."[21]

Alan Greenspan and Clinton's treasury secretary Robert Rubin feared a systemic meltdown if LTCM declared bankruptcy. They understood that complex derivatives linked LTCM to major banks and traders all over the globe. If LTCM went down, it could set off a domino effect leading to bank failures. Still, the Fed refused to bail the hedge fund out, fearing that this would create a moral hazard. Every hedge fund would gamble more recklessly if they knew that they too might be "too big to fail." Instead the Fed pressured a consortium of fourteen major banks that had lent to LTCM to put up $3.6 billion to bail them out and take over the failed fund. The international meltdown was averted.

Having seen the best and brightest fail with derivatives, you would think that Greenspan and Rubin would have called for regulating the shadowy derivatives market. You would be wrong.

––––––––

Unlike Alan Greenspan, Brooksley Born is not a household name. She should be. She had the chutzpah as head of the Commodities and Futures Trading Commission to call for regulating derivatives, in defiance of Greenspan and Rubin.

Ms. Born, a teacher's daughter whose father was the head of a public-welfare agency in San Francisco, had attended Stanford University in the late 1950s and early 1960s. It was a time when talented women had great difficulty finding meaningful careers. She had wanted to be a doctor, but her guidance counselor told her she should be a nurse. If she didn't want to do that, it showed she lacked compassion and she should switch away from the helping professions. Born became an English major. But once she learned how hard it would be to find a job that used her English degree she entered Stanford Law School.

In 1962, Born was one of 10 women in a class of 165. Some of the men weren't pleased: "At the beginning of my first year, one of the men in my class told me I was doing a terrible thing because I had taken the place of a man who had to go to Vietnam and might get killed. That was difficult to deal with. At the time males were drafted if they were unable to get a deferment."[22]

Upon graduation she clerked for a liberal federal judge and then became an associate at Arnold and Porter in Washington, DC. She admired the firm because it had vigorously defended victims of McCarthyism during the 1950s. As a lawyer she developed an interest in international trade—which eventually included defending international clients in suits about derivatives—and in women's issues. She taught one of the first "Women and Law" classes in the DC area and seemed to have a great deal of respect for unions and collective bargaining. (She also became involved in the litigation surrounding the Hunt brothers' efforts to corner the silver market, made famous in the hilarious movie *Trading Places*.) Born was an ideal candidate for public service in the Clinton administration.

In 1995, the chair of the Commodities Futures Trading Commission opened up and Born got the nod. The position put her smack in the middle of the derivatives debate. Unlike so many congressional members and staff, she actually knew how they worked. It was a fortuitous appointment.

The last Reagan appointee to hold the job was Wendy Gramm, wife of Senator Phil Gramm, the Texas Republican. In her last act as chair, Gramm had granted an official regulatory exemption allowing the trading of derivatives in unregulated over-the-counter markets. In effect she cut the ribbon on the derivatives casino. As Born describes it, "The market was completely opaque. Neither the commission nor any other federal regulator knew what was going on in that market!"

Born was at the helm of the Commodities Futures Trading Commission when Long-Term Capital Management failed. As she said, it "had to be bailed out by a number of large OTC derivatives dealers because it had $1.25 trillion worth of derivative contracts at the same time it had less than $4 billion in capital to support them." (In other words, it was on the hook for $312.50 for every $1 it actually had of its own.)

All Born's training and experience warned her that this was "a nightmare waiting to happen," as she put it in 2003. "I realized there was a tremendous potential danger to the markets in the United States and to the international economy." So she tiptoed oh so carefully toward oversight for derivatives, a question she believed was well within her purview. She recalled that "The commission came out with a concept release in the *Federal Register* asking for input from the industry and other interested people concerning the need for more oversight of the over-the-counter derivatives market." In other words, she was ready to consider reversing Wendy Gramm's exemption.

She might as well have threatened to nuke Wall Street. The response from the derivatives industry, from Fed chair Alan Greenspan, from Arthur Levitt, head of the Securities and Exchange Commission, and even from the kindly treasury secretary, Robert Rubin, was swift and harsh. According to the *New York Times*,

> On April 21, 1998, senior federal financial regulators convened in a wood-paneled conference room at the Treasury to discuss Ms. Born's proposal. Mr. Rubin and Mr. Greenspan implored her to reconsider, according to both Mr. Greenberger [a senior director of the CFTC] and Mr. Levitt.
>
> Ms. Born pushed ahead. On June 5, 1998, Mr. Greenspan, Mr. Rubin and Mr. Levitt called on Congress to prevent Ms. Born from acting until more senior regulators developed their own recommendations. Mr. Levitt says he now regrets that decision. Mr. Greenspan and Mr. Rubin were "joined at the hip on this," he said. "They were certainly very fiercely opposed to this and persuaded me that this would cause chaos. . . ."
>
> Greenspan told Brooksley that she essentially didn't know what she was doing and she'd cause a financial crisis," said Michael Greenberger, who was a senior director at the commission. "Brooksley was this woman who was not playing tennis with these guys and not

having lunch with these guys. There was a little bit of the feeling that this woman was not of Wall Street."[23]

Then, to finally kill any effort to control OTC derivatives, Senator Phil Gramm successfully inserted an amendment into a 1999 appropriations bill that postponed all CFTC regulatory efforts for six months. There were no hearings, no discussions. A year later, Gramm attached a last-minute 232-page amendment to the omnibus appropriations bill called the "Commodities Futures Modernization Act." He seemed to be the only member of Congress who understood it. On the Senate floor Gramm argued that the bill, which exempted derivatives from all regulations, would "protect financial institutions from overregulation" and "position our financial services industries to be world leaders into the new century."[24] It passed and President Clinton signed it. The bill was viewed as a sop to Enron, which was deep into the derivatives business. Wendy Gramm went on Enron's board and made a million or so. Brooksley Born departed from the government, retired from her law firm, and continued her work in support of women's issues in the Washington, DC, area.

Before we so unceremoniously dismiss Greenspan's love of all things private and derivative, we need to ask a critical question. Would the kind of regulatory reform Born had in mind have prevented the current financial meltdown?

Born wanted increased transparency—a kiss-and-tell policy that would have enabled all investors to figure out who had what kind of derivative relationships with whom. She also wanted to be sure traders and dealers were openly and honestly conducting their business, and that the books accurately reflected the assets and liabilities involved in these complex transactions. But she didn't want to kill the derivatives market. "These instruments," she said, "can be used to reduce economic risk, and they are certainly very valuable and useful economic instruments."[25] She just wanted to prevent them from creating "enormous risks"—as they had at Long-Term Capital Management, and soon would at Enron.

Buried within Greenspan's ideological gibberish is a compelling practical argument: This kind of regulatory regime would not work even if it were desirable. He and many others believe that derivatives are so pliable that they would immediately be reconstructed to circumvent any rules we passed to regulate them. The evil genius of derivatives is that they can be packaged, repackaged, stripped, striped, sliced, and glued back together in an almost infinite number of sizes and shapes. It would be hard ever to make them entirely transparent. Even if we reined in derivatives in this country, it would be difficult to prevent some small country from becoming a new haven for derivative trading, because the payoff would be enormous: trillions of dollars of deals. So unless you could round up the entire world to regulate derivatives, they would probably find ways to scramble back into the shadows. It's very hard to police financial relations (or betting) among consenting adults.

This argument has some merit. It seems likely that derivative traders would find a way to evade the mild regulatory approach suggested by the GAO and Born. The powerful derivatives-industry lobbyists would probably be able to secure plenty of caveats in any such regulations. "Protect Financial Innovation" would have been the fight song in Congress. It's highly possible that Born's efforts, however laudable, would have been far too accommodating and therefore ineffective.

Surely letting derivatives roam free was a recipe for disaster. But controlling them would require a great deal of political will. We'd have to see an awful lot of derivatives-derived havoc to generate that kind of will. It would take . . . a system meltdown. Like now.

Now that our biggest banks, largest insurance company, and largest mortgage agencies have been essentially nationalized, the time is ripe for extensive regulatory reform. But there are nagging questions that may not be so easily resolved. What if there is a fundamental underlying tendency in capitalism that leads toward asset inflation and booms, and then crashes? Can carefully crafted regulations really address such problems? We'll return to these themes in the concluding chapters. But now it's time to don our hazmat suits and take a closer look at Wall Street's toxic waste.

six

Getting the Story Backwards

THE 2008 ECONOMIC CRISIS is desperate for culprits. Was it Wall Street fat cats and their $100-million bonuses and retirement packages? Predatory mortgage brokers who lent money recklessly? Hedge fund speculators who took enormous leveraged bets? Alan Greenspan and the Fed who failed to regulate? Subprime borrowers who tried to buy homes they couldn't afford? Or how about the rest of us, who piled up debt on multiple credit cards? (The Wisconsin folks might also add a few desperado banks and investment houses to the list.)

When faced with such a catastrophic and complex set of events, the media defaults to a misery-loves-company collective narrative: "We're all to blame." We all lived beyond our means and now we're paying the price. From the elite billionaire hedge fund operator to the poor schmo with no equity who thought he could gamble on a $400,000 home, we all lived too high on the hog. In Wisconsin the collective tale of woe might run from the retired school employees who thought they had earned their medical benefits to the school board officials who wanted to get into the Wall Street scams, to the brokers, banks, and investment houses who hoodwinked the local school boards. In every locale, it's time each of us takes full responsibility for our profligate ways. Repent, ye sinners, repent!

The narrative has appeal. When we feel a collective hurt, it is soothing to share it during times of crisis. But this story never happened. We may have been living beyond our means, but very few of us had anything to do with the meltdown or the financial toxic waste that is polluting the economy. While many of us may enjoy an occasional game of penny-ante poker, only the elite can play fantasy finance.

But wait, what about the bursting housing bubble, which set off this whole crisis? Wasn't it caused by marginal buyers who got mortgages even though they had no way to pay them off? And didn't those big government-sponsored mortgage agencies, Freddie Mac and Fannie Mae, let those low-income buyers in?

Conservatives are pushing this line of attack, which conveniently preserves their free-market ideology. The culprit was government—once again!

Their case starts by pointing the finger directly at Democrats, who supposedly pressured mortgage lenders to relax standards for lower-income minority buyers. In this scenario, guilty liberal politicians first passed the ill-advised Community Reinvestment Act in 1977 to force banks to give mortgages to low-income minorities, and then pressured Freddie Mac and Fannie Mae to buy up these risky mortgages.

Larry Kudlow, CNBC's free-market apostle, spelled it all out for MSNBC's Joe Scarborough, the former Republican congressman from Florida. (Full disclosure: In 1970 Larry and I worked together in Connecticut, along with Bill Clinton, in a losing effort to elect anti–Vietnam War candidate Joseph Duffey to the U.S. Senate. At the time Kudlow seemed liberal while palling around with pinkos.)

> *Kudlow*: It's time for the Congress, Republicans and Democrats to stop encouraging—exhorting and forcing banks to make low-income loans with no documentation. Stop that—literally pushed these lenders to make-low income loans.
>
> *Scarborough*: Hold on a second. You cannot blame this on low-income people that are getting a house.
>
> *Kudlow*: I'm not blaming them. . . . Subprime, substandard loans were a creature of the U.S. Congress in the '90s and the 2000s.

Scarborough: Are you saying that poor people have caused this crisis?

Kudlow: Not poor people. Members of Congress who were rich people. But their liberal guilt consciences forced banks and lenders to make lousy substandard loans and that has to be repealed. . . . Not everybody can afford a home, Joe. Some people have to rent. . .

Scarborough: That was Larry Kudlow of CNBC's *Kudlow and Company*, 7 p.m. tonight where you'll also learn on that show that it was the poor people who were also responsible for the Kennedy assassination. [laughter][1]

Let's start with the Community Reinvestment Act (CRA). There is scant evidence that it has had a substantial impact on the housing bubble and bust, let alone on the broader economy. The Act did indeed ask banks to make more loans to low-income community residents. The bill was designed to stop de-facto discrimination, called "red-lining," which disqualified entire neighborhoods from receiving loans. Minority applicants from those neighborhoods were denied mortgages even when they had better financial qualifications than comparable buyers in white neighborhoods. Before the House Committee on Financial Services on February 13, 2008, law professor Michael S. Barr, a former Clinton administration Treasury official, put CRA's role in perspective:

> More than half of subprime loans were made by independent mortgage companies not subject to comprehensive federal supervision; another 30 percent of such originations were made by affiliates of banks or thrifts, which are not subject to routine examination or supervision, and the remaining 20 percent were made by banks and thrifts. Although reasonable people can disagree about how to interpret the evidence, my own judgment is that the worst and most widespread abuses occurred in the institutions with the least federal oversight.[2]

Janet L. Yellen, president of the Federal Reserve Bank of San Francisco, also recognized a distinct difference between CRA lending and the subprime housing crisis. On March 31, 2008, she said:

> There has been a tendency to conflate the current problems in the subprime market with CRA-motivated lending, or with lending to low-income families in general. I believe it is very important to make a distinction between the two. Most of the loans made by depository institutions examined under the CRA have not been higher-priced loans, and studies have shown that the CRA has increased the volume of responsible lending to low- and moderate-income households.[3]

Traiger & Hinckley LLP, a law firm that advises financial institutions on CRA compliance, also finds no evidence that CRA contributed to the subprime crisis. In their third annual analysis of publicly available home-purchase mortgage-lending data, they write, "Our study concludes that CRA *Banks were substantially less likely than other lenders to make the kinds of risky home purchase loans that helped fuel the foreclosure crisis*" (emphasis in the original).[4]

The heaviest artillery conservatives fire against Freddie Mac and Fannie Mae comes from "The Last Trillion-Dollar Commitment," written by Peter J. Wallison and Charles W. Calomiris for the American Enterprise Institute. The authors argue that the whole idea behind Freddie and Fannie is flawed. The government created them to facilitate home ownership by buying mortgages from local banks and mortgage companies and then selling them as securities to investors. And yet they are (were) private operations with stockholders and CEOs who sought to maximize shareholder returns and CEO compensation. Because they had the tacit backing of the federal government, Fannie and Freddie could secure cheaper funding in the capital markets and therefore had an unfair advantage over firms in the private sector. The authors contend that Fanny and Freddie took too many risks because they knew that in a pinch, the government would bail them out (and it did).

The authors claim that Freddie and Fannie—the giants of the mortgage field—got the whole financial crisis rolling back in 2004, when they first began investing heavily in junk mortgages. They write, "It is likely that this huge increase in commitments to junk lending was largely the result of signals from Fannie and Freddie that they were ready to buy these loans in bulk."[5] Boom. The race was on and major financial intermediaries around the world got into the act. And then it all came crashing down.

Wallison and Calomiris argue that Fannie and Freddie fundamentally distorted the market. "The special relationship with Congress was [Fannie's and Freddie's] undoing because it allowed them to escape the market discipline—the wariness of lenders—that keeps corporate managements from taking unacceptable risks."

National Journal columnist Stuart Taylor put it more starkly. He writes that Wallison and Calomiris showed that "Fannie and Freddie appear to have played a major role in causing the current crisis, in part because their quasi-governmental status violated basic principles of a healthy free enterprise system by allowing them to privatize profit while socializing risk."[6]

The *Washington Post* editorial board goes one step further: "We are not witnessing a crisis of the free market but a crisis of distorted markets."[7]

Free markets good. Government interference bad. Freddie and Fannie, the nation's biggest mortgage buyers, were pressured by liberals to bring the American dream to poor people. And because they "escaped the market discipline . . . that keeps corporate managements from taking unacceptable risks," they agreed to give mortgages to those who had no business buying homes. Everyone who invested in these mortgages got shafted; they had to sell the houses on the cheap to recoup some of their losses.

And this brought down entire neighborhoods as housing values crashed. Foreclosures spread. Financial institutions and investors suffered more losses, banks and investment houses collapsed. The whole banking system teetered. Credit froze and then the entire economy tanked. And it's all the government's fault—especially Kudlow's bleeding-heart liberals.

Not quite. Wallison, Calomiris, and company have it backwards. "Market discipline" did not tame "corporate management from taking on unacceptable risks." The financial industry fiercely competed to create the wildest casino ever: the bigger the risks, the bigger the profits. Market discipline (the competitive drive for profits) drove them forward rather than held them back. Free-market ideologues can't handle the obvious: unregulated financial markets crashed *on their own*, and are threatening to take all of us down with them. In fact, free-market discipline failed so calamitously that the freedom-loving Bush administration had to socialize much of the banking system. Talk about eating crow!

As for Fannie and Freddie, they did not cause our current meltdown. And the bad mortgages they bought were not the result of either the Community Reinvestment Act or their lack of exposure to market forces. This is not to say that Fannie and Freddie were paragons of public virtue. They were a mess. But if anything, market pressures drove them to join the derivative casino. They didn't invent it.

Deconstructing a few esoteric lines from Wallison and Calomiris' indictment of Fannie and Freddie might help lead us to the real culprits.

> Without [Fannie's and Freddie's] commitment to
> purchase the AAA tranches [slices] of these securitiza-
> tions, it is unlikely that the pools [of subprime mort-
> gages] could have been formed and marketed around
> the world. . . . Accordingly not only did [they] destroy
> their own financial condition with their excessive

purchases of subprime loans in the three-year period of
2005–2007, but they also played a major role in weakening or destroying the solvency and stability of other
financial institutions and investors in the United States
and abroad.[8]

Consider the colossal contradiction contained in this passage:
How can something have an AAA rating (the highest, safest
debt rating provided by the credit agencies) and at the same time
be connected to "subprime loans"? An AAA-rated security is
supposed to be very, very safe and should have posed absolutely
no problem to Fannie, Freddie, or any other investor around the
globe. But if it was really subprime junk, how did it get a triple-A
rating? Fannie and Freddie can be justly blamed for many indis-
cretions, but how can you blame them for buying AAA-rated
securities?

Well, my hedge fund source informs me that "by this time,
people already knew that the ratings were complete bunk." So
Fannie and Freddie should have known that they were gambling
and not making sound investments. This is no doubt true. But as
economist Dean Baker states in his excellent account of the crisis,
"It's important to point out that Fannie and Freddie followed the
private sector into this area. In fact, they lost market share to the
private-sector in this area."[9]

But there's a larger conceptual problem that the Kudlow
conservatives choose not to address. The entire subprime mortgage market totals "only" $1.3 trillion—about 2 percent of our
nation's household net worth. Credible estimates for the losses
incurred owing to subprime loans and the next riskiest class
of loans, "Alt-A," together total about $300 billion (divided
equally between the two types of risky loans).[10] How could that
amount devastate the world economy? Or look at it this way:
If the potential high-risk mortgage defaults totaled only $300
billion, then surely the trillion-dollar federal bank bailouts would
have covered the entire problem, and then some. But they didn't.

No, something else far more powerful and insidious was at work, and the clues hide in those AAA securities that were created out of junk debt.

What are they? Why did they go bust? And how did they crash the financial system?

———

As we entered the twenty-first century, the economy experienced severe stresses and strains. The dot.com bubble inflated and burst, and then 9/11 hit. As the economy slid into recession, Alan Greenspan's Fed responded by dramatically lowering interest rates. Many believe this overstimulated the housing sector. It certainly opened vast new vistas for derivatives. Greenspan, who had already beaten back attempts to regulate derivatives, was supremely confident that financial free markets could police themselves. Referring to this period, he wrote in his memoirs, "The worst [derivatives] have failed; investors no longer fund them and are not likely to in the future."[11]

Unfortunately for us, this was not Greenspan's most prescient observation. The worst derivatives were about to latch onto the housing boom like the creature in *Alien*.

When interest rates go down significantly, especially long-term rates, mortgage rates go down. This, in turn, increases the demand for homes. With lower interest rates, you get lower monthly mortgage payments, so you can more easily afford your first home, a better home, or a second home. It's also easier to find buyers for your existing home. At the same time, lower interest rates help home builders finance their projects thereby increasing the supply of houses.

What's more, when interest rates go down, the value of assets increases. I always found that a bit strange, but here's the example I tell myself to make it clearer. Let's say you own a 30-year, $10,000 government bond that pays 6 percent. That means it provides you with $600 each year in interest payments. Imagine that long-term interest rates fall dramatically, and now the government is selling 30-year bonds with a 3 percent interest coupon. So the new $10,000 bonds will only provide $300 a year in interest payments. Obviously, your old 30-year bond is now a lot more valuable. In fact your old bond (depending on how close to maturity it is) would probably fetch more like $20,000 (since 3 percent of $20,000 = $600). So that asset is definitely up in value. A house also is an asset, and declining interest rates increase its value as well. And when asset values rise, we feel richer and are willing to spend more. When people see their homes go up in value, they take out more home-equity loans to remodel the kitchen, buy a new car, or send the kids to college.

So put it all together—very low mortgage rates, low interest rates for builders, rising home values, and increased demand for homes—and you have the makings of a housing boom. But that does not fully explain the explosion in housing prices that started just before the turn of the century.

While the rest of us saw just a housing boom, the derivatives industry saw a gold-plated casino, the biggest one ever. The world was about to become their private Las Vegas. They were more than ready for the action since they had already packaged a set of derivative games perfectly suited for the housing casino.

Financial innovations come about to solve specific financial problems. Here was the problem. A bank loans you money so you can buy a house. The bank gets an upfront fee (usually from 1 to 3 percent of the total mortgage, referred to as points), a very nice revenue for the bank or mortgage company. Then the bank gets principal and interest payments back from you each month over the next 15 or 30 years. That's a very long time to tie up the bank's money. The bank would prefer to get those loans off their books so that they can issue more and more mortgages and earn the juicy up-front points. That's where the real money is for the bank. Waiting around for the principal and interest to come in isn't nearly as lucrative. So the idea is to get rid of the loan—to sell it off to someone else.

During the Depression when the housing market had ground

to a standstill, the New Deal (not the private sector) created the financial machinery to solve this problem. It established Fannie Mae in 1934, and it bought up local banks' mortgage loans—so long as the borrower had a decent income, a good job record, and a substantial down payment.[12] The originating bank continued to service the loan, collecting the mortgage payments on behalf of Fannie Mae. But the loan was no longer on the local bank's books, so the bank had more capital to loan out again. Fannie Mae then sold the loans to investors, with a federal guarantee that the loans would be paid back even if the homeowner defaulted.

Twenty years later, the federal government invented another key instrument—mortgage-backed securities. These were developed for mortgages arranged by government agencies like the Veterans Administration and the Office of Public and Indian Housing. To more efficiently sell these loans to investors, in 1968 Congress set up a new agency, the Government National Mortgage Association (Ginny Mae). It pooled all these government-backed loans and chopped them up into securities. (*Security* is just another word to describe a financial instrument, one that is transferable and has value because of its income flow; *securitization* is the process of creating these securities from income flows that previously could not be easily bought and sold. Each pool of thousands of mortgages could be chopped up into hundreds of individual securities.) Ginny Mae then sold the securities to investors, all backed by the federal government. Each pool contained thousands of single-family loans that conformed to good government lending standards. Every slice of what Ginny Mae offered from a given pool was identical—and Ginny Mae paid back each investor's share of the returned principal with a set interest rate.[13]

This was problematic for some investors—you didn't know how long the security would last because sometimes the underlying mortgages would be paid back early. If interest rates declined many homeowners would rush to refinance. When they did, that mortgage would leave the Ginny Mae pool and the investors would get back their share of the remaining principal immediately. You wouldn't lose any money, but many investors wanted to know exactly how long their investments would last.

This uncertainty provided an opening for traders. They soon created financial products (derivatives) that more or less pulled Ginny Mae interest payments and principal payments apart. For a fee, you could buy a Ginny Mae derivative that gave you a fixed rate of interest for a fixed period of time, or you could buy into the principal payments, essentially taking a bet on how fast the homes refinanced.

It was just a short hop, skip, and jump for derivative dealers to see that there was a huge mortgage market out there that had nothing to do with the federal government. Specifically, there were marginal buyers whose mortgages were not prime ("A-paper"), but rather "Alt-A" (for Alternative A-paper, a little riskier than prime) or even subprime. These buyers didn't qualify for federal subsidies, and weren't included in Freddie and Fannie's mainstream federal loan repurchases.

Ah ha! Marginal buyers = higher interest rates = higher fees. Very appealing, especially in an era of declining interest rates—provided the risk of default could be contained. Why not borrow Ginny Mae's strategy for these more marginal buyers? If we can pool these risky loans and "securitize" them, we can sell the pieces to investors all over the world. Derivative dealers could make money by forming and selling the securities, and by trading them in a secondary market. No doubt financial engineering geniuses could use them as a platform to derive more and more derivatives so that hungry investors could do some additional speculating.

But, on second thought, simply copying the Ginny Mae format wouldn't do. Because these subprime pools would be risky, the new mortgage-backed securities, unlike Ginny Mae securities, would never be rated AAA (the highest rating). And of course they wouldn't have the government's backing.

Subprime mortgages were just too risky. In fact they were more or less the equivalent of junk bonds—a very speculative investment. And this would limit the investor market. Many institutional investors are prohibited from making large investments in speculative securities. For example, pension funds, insurance companies, and banks often are restricted to purchasing securities with at least "investment grade" ratings, and explicitly prohibited from buying anything with junk status (meaning they are too risky to receive a rating). So pooling the subprime mortgages just wouldn't do. Back to the drawing board.

Enter the financial engineering geniuses. First there was a fellow named Larry Fink, who in 1983 worked with a team at First Boston Bank on behalf of Freddie Mac. Fink came up with an invention called a collateralized mortgage obligation (CMO), designed to work with a pool of low-risk mortgages that conformed to Freddie and Fannie standards.

Author Satyajit Das claims that "Michael Milken, the junk bond king, created the first CDO [collateralized debt obligation] in 1987 at now-defunct Drexel Burnham Lambert Inc."[14] He expanded Fink's idea to work with a pool of junk bonds. It quickly turned into a humongous winner . . . until becoming a world-record-breaking loser. (Please listen up all you folks from Whitefish Bay, Kenosha, Kimberly, Waukesha, and West Allis–West Milwaukee. This is where your story really starts.)

Here was the idea. Let's gather together these marginal subprime mortgages into big pools. But when we slice up each pool into securities, unlike at Ginny Mae, we'll slice them up *unequally*. We'll chop up the pool so that *risk and the rate of return varies by slice*. We'll design some of the pieces so that they are very secure while others will be far riskier. The more secure pieces will get lower rates of return and the very risky pieces will get much higher rates of return.

How is that possible? First and foremost, you've got to add some continental charm and sophistication to your nomenclature.

Instead of slices, the derivatives industry adopted the French word for slice—*tranche*. Sounds more secure already! Next comes the imaginative financial engineering.

Imagine a pool of a thousand subprime mortgages—a large collection of loans backed by homes whose buyers have less than stellar credit ratings. They might not have made a down payment on their home—they might not even have a job. Every month most of them, actually nearly all of them, will still make their mortgage payment. People don't like to lose their houses, even if they can't really afford them. Every once in a while, someone in the pool will default, but the historical record shows that more than 85 percent of the people will keep on paying. So this large pool as a whole will generate each month a robust flow of income from the mortgage payments.

The clever derivative folks figured out that you can create securities from that pool that have very different amounts of risk. Here's a very simple example.[15]

Let's slice that pool into three tranches of securities—high, medium, and low. We give the securities in the high tranche (called the senior tranche or super-senior tranche) first dibs on *all* the interest payments coming out of the pool. To really protect the investors who buy securities from this highest tranche, you can set it up so the senior tranche would get interest payments even if the default rate were several times the historical average for subprime borrowers. So by giving senior tranche first claim on all the interest payments from the entire pool of subprime loans, you've taken away much of the risk for the investors who bought senior tranche securities.

Your middle tranche (called the mezzanine tranche, naturally) would be slightly less protected; it would have to absorb losses if the default rate hit maybe two times the historical average. Securities drawn from the mezzanine tranche would have more risk than the senior tranche but would still be much safer than investing in the pool as a whole.

Finally, you've got your bottom tranche (called the equity

tranche because equity—aka corporate stock shares—in case of bankruptcy, also has the lowest and last claim on assets). This tranche takes the first hit on defaults. It is saddled with the bulk of the risk of the entire pool.

Since the risk varies for each tranche, the rates of return also vary. The senior tranche, being the safest, would get a lower rate of return. The mezzanine would get a higher rate, and the equity tranche would get an enormous rate of return—20, 30, or even 40 percent per year (so long as defaults on the underlying mortgages stay low)—because it was shouldering nearly all of the risk for the entire pool.

Here's a visual analogy.[16] Imagine a wine bottle and an upside-down pyramid of wine glasses with three levels. The top layer has seven glasses, the middle has two, and the bottom just one. The wine bottle is the pool of subprime mortgages. The wine in the bottle is the sum of all the interest payments from the subprime mortgages. Each wine glass in our upside-down pyramid represents a financial security that is sold to investors. Each row is a tranche. You start pouring the wine (interest) from the top down to pay the investors. The senior tranche is the top row and it gets the first servings of wine. The middle row, the mezzanine tranche, gets served next, and the bottom glass in the equity tranche is last to be served.

If some of the subprime mortgages backing the CDO default, there is less wine to be poured for all the glasses, but the top glasses are first in line to get filled to the brim. If the wine runs out before it reaches the bottom-tranche glass, too bad—that's the risk you take when you buy that glass.

So far so good, but not good enough. To build a massive global market for the top tranche of wine glasses, you need to get high ratings from one of the three major ratings agencies: Moody's, Standard and Poor's, or Fitch's. If you could get one of them to give you AAA ratings for the senior tranche, you could market it to pension funds, insurance companies, banks, and the like. Big, big money.

SUBPRIME MORTGAGE WINE

Senior Tranche

Mezzanine Tranche

Equity Tranche ("Toxic Waste")

That is precisely what happened. Derivative houses were able to convince the rating agencies that the top tranche was supersafe and should be rated AAA, virtually as good as you can get without being backed by the federal government. How they pulled this off is a longer story that we'll return to later. But for now all we need to know is that the derivative bankers secured AAA ratings for the top tranche. They also secured decent investment-grade ratings for the mezzanine tranches. The lowly equity tranche, however, got stuck with junk-bond status.

From the start, the derivative dealers called it "nuclear waste" and "toxic waste."

In theory this makes some sense. Our top row of wine glasses is protected by the two rows below it. It would take many failures within the wine bottle for there not to be enough wine to fill the top tranche of glasses. However, the creators of these securities also wanted there to be as many wine glasses in the top row as possible, and they wanted them rated AAA—which is what happened. They were remarkably successful in getting AAA ratings for the entire top row—up to 80 percent of all the securities in a CDO. Nice work.

Here's the kicker: Not only were the senior tranches rated AAA, but they came with a *higher* rate of return than other sorts of AAA securities (like GE or AIG AAA-rated bonds). So the top row of glasses became hot commodities for investors from the northern tip of Norway to the eastern shores of Wisconsin. A massive global market opened up for derivative dealers.

Let's pause to admire the true alchemy of this financial engineering. You take a bunch of subprime mortgages from marginal borrowers, and you put them in a big pool (your wine bottle). You divide up the pool into securities (your wine glasses), but you don't divide them up equally. Each tranche (row of wine glasses) gets a different rate of return based on how much risk it assumes. Because the top tranche assumes relatively little risk, it gets a lower return, but also gets rated AAA—and it has a higher interest-rate coupon than other AAA securities. Kind of amazing, given that none of the mortgages in the pool either on their own or bundled together could possibly earn such a rating. After all, each mortgage in the pool is risky, far below Freddie Mac standards.

Yet with a bit of French vocabulary and fancy wine pouring, our financial engineers turned a very large chunk of the pool (75 percent or more of it) into AAA-rated securities. It's a miracle. This new derivative, which generically is called a collateralized debt obligation (CDO)[17]—which includes all the tranches—

turned about three-quarters of the sow's ear into a highly profitable silk purse.[18]

What about the risky equity tranches—the bottom row of glasses that might stay dry? You would think no one would want to drink from a glass labeled "toxic waste." You would be wrong. The potential high returns for the equity tranches were so alluring that often the originating bank held on to them, or sold them at a profit to speculators who lined up for them. They even pawned them off on pension funds. The largest investment houses and banks (like now-defunct Bear Stearns, Merrill Lynch, and Wachovia, and others who survived) engaged in a highly successful and profitable campaign to unload billions of dollars of subprime equity tranches onto state pension funds covering public employees.[19] According to "The Poison in Your Pension," a Bloomberg Markets report issued in July 2007, state pension funds purchased 18 percent of the riskiest CDO equity tranches, but only 4 percent of the higher AAA-rated tranches.[20] You can bet there now are some empty wine glasses in those pension funds.

For a while the wine flowed freely. During the housing boom the mortgage-default rate was extremely low, even for subprime borrowers. And with home prices rising, subprime-mortgage holders expected to get most of their money back even if the house had to be foreclosed and sold. So for aggressive investors, at least in the short run, the equity tranche seemed more than worth the risk. If defaults started to inch up, the banks figured they would be the first to spot it and could unload the toxic waste before it polluted their books. And as we'll see in a bit, you could even buy derivative insurance to reduce the risk of the equity tranches.

If your eyes are glazed over from all this wine, just remember one important point: this was a money machine for the derivatives industry. The alchemists walked away with billions of dollars in fees for organizing the pools, creating the securities, marketing them, trading them, and collecting the big returns from the equity tranches. We don't know what percentage of bank profits came from these derivatives, but we can be sure that it was high—amounting to tens of billions of dollars. Traders got enormous bonuses. Their bosses got a nice piece. Many golden parachutes—those robust executive retirement packages—were stitched together with CDO profits.

This wasn't just wine. It was Dom Perignon.

We now should know enough to kiss goodbye the fairy tale about how those greedy, reckless subprime borrowers or the big, bad Freddie/Fannie agencies drove us into the ditch. They did not create this derivative bonanza.

The CDOs—and the process that created them—were so profitable they generated enormous demand for subprime mortgages among profit-hungry CDO packagers. In fact they propelled a global conveyer belt of subprime mortgages. Investors all over wanted the higher returns offered through the CDO tranches. Derivative dealers in banks rushed to fill the demand by creating the new securities, sucking up all the subprime mortgages they could get their hands on. Mortgage companies out in the field knew that they could quickly sell the loans they wrote so they scrambled to find clients. After all, the more loans they wrote the more fees they would earn. Besides, it made economic sense to offer a wide variety of loan products that would allow all kinds of people to buy homes. Adjustable rates, teaser rates, no income verification, no down payments, interest only, interest tacked on to the principal, predatory loans, loans to dead people—it didn't matter as long as the mortgage broker got the closing fee and could pass on the mortgage to a CDO packager immediately.[21] It didn't matter if the borrower's application was science fiction. No one was checking. Let 'er rip.

This demand for more subprime mortgages for the CDO pools naturally lured more marginal buyers into the market and increased demand for houses. And of course, many of these buyers were eager to take advantage of the lax standards. This increased home prices and encouraged more home building. What if the homebuyer couldn't make his monthly payment? Not a problem. Prices were rising quickly. Even if the mortgage went into default, the home could be resold for as much as or more than the outstanding loan.

It was so American: The casino was pumping out enormous profits for the derivative gang. Speculators were buying and selling houses and raking in the bucks. And even low-income homebuyers got a peek at the Promised Land.

But not for long.

seven

Financial Weapons of Mass Destruction

To FINANCIAL ENGINEERS, CDO derivatives are gorgeous. They can be twisted and turned into a million tantalizing shapes. One beauty is called a "CDO squared." You've got a bunch of high-risk CDO equity tranches that just aren't selling. So what do you do? You make more wine. You pour all those bottom-tranche glasses into a new bottle. Then you create another upside-down pyramid of glasses, and sell them, with your wine pouring, from the top down. (The idea is to gather up hundreds of bottom-tranche wine glasses from many different CDOs, so that you'll have enough wine for a new bottle. In theory, they shouldn't all go dry at the same time.) With a little bit of guile, luck, and some fancy mathematical modeling that befuddles the all-too-willing rating agencies, you've created a high-rated, highly marketable new set of senior tranche securities—all based on the junk of the junk.

Pretty cool. But what if you can't sell all the bottom tranches of the CDO-squared securities? You guessed it. You form another pool of those untouchables—called a CDO cubed—and tranche away again. If you're not too tipsy, let's walk slowly through this winery. You started by taking the *bottom* glasses of wine from many CDOs and pouring them into a new bottle. Then that bottle of risky CDO wine is used to pour a new upside-down pyramid of glasses—your CDO squared. Then you take the bottom glasses of many CDO-squared pyramids and pour these very, very risky glasses of wine into a new bottle that fills up yet another upside-down pyramid of glasses—the CDO cubed. Anyone buying this stuff is either very drunk or nuts or both. (Fortunately, there are very few cubed CDOs.)

But the real wizardry comes with the addition of one more incredibly seductive derivative: the credit default swap (CDS). (Dear Wisconsin: This is the critical component of the garbage they sold to your school districts.)

Credit default swaps. Warren Buffet called them "financial weapons of mass destruction." Attach them to your CDOs, spew this potion of toxic tranches all over the globe, and presto: The crash of 2008.

Credit default swaps were added to CDOs to solve a specific financial problem—the time and effort it took to form a CDO, called the "ramp-up." To form a regular CDO, you have to get legal title to the one thousand or so subprime mortgages (or credit card debts or car leases or corporate loans or bonds). This takes time and a lot of legal fees. You don't want to tie up your bank's money for three or four months. In that time, the financial world could turn against you before you can unload the tranches. There must be a faster, simpler way.

There is. The particular swap that solves this problem is viewed most clearly with corporate bonds, the heart of the swap market.

Corporate bonds are in essence a loan to a corporation. You give the company money and it gives you a bond—a piece of paper that says they agree to pay you interest for a period of time. After that, you get your principal back in full . . . provided the company doesn't fold in the meantime. Each kind of corporate bond gets a risk rating (from the rating companies) based on the financial health and strength of the company. The lower the risk, the better the rating and the less interest the corporation needs to pay to attract investors to purchase its bonds. If the company goes bankrupt, corporate bondholders are first in line to get repaid from the remaining corporate assets. So bonds often retain considerable value even if the corporation goes under.

Now let's say you bought $100 million of Lehman Brothers bonds back in 2006 when they were high flyers on Wall Street. Even though these bonds seemed solid, you might have desired a bit of insurance, just to be sure. So you asked your friendly banker to write you a credit default swap. For a fee from you (let's say $500,000 per year for five years—0.5 percent), you could buy full protection for the $100-million principal of your bond in case Lehman Brothers defaulted during that time. You're willing to pay it, even though it cuts into your interest payments from the bonds, because the credit default swap secures your principal entirely. It makes your balance sheet look less risky and helps your company maintain a good debt rating. You've transferred the risk through the swap to whoever sold you the insurance.

Why would someone else take on that risk? Because they are betting that it is unlikely that such a prestigious Wall Street firm would fail, and the $500,000 per year in fees they would collect from you seemed adequate to cover that small risk. And besides, the bank or other investor who is buying your risk gets these nice premiums without putting out any of their own money. That's a nice return. Everyone is happy.

It turns out that thousands of investors and institutions thought this type of hedging was a spectacular deal. The next step was to marry the credit default swap and the collateralized debt obligation into a *synthetic CDO*—precisely what the Wisconsin folks bought.

The first synthetic CDOs were invented in 1997 by Bill Demchak and his group at JPMorgan. They were searching for a way to protect their bank from the billions of dollars in outstanding loans they had made to their traditional customers—other large companies, banks, and foreign governments. They didn't want to sell the loans because that might upset their customers who had long, established relationships with the bank. So Demchak and his group invented a way *to get rid of the risk but not the loans*. They set up a pool of credit default swaps on three hundred corporate loans that JPMorgan held. Those swaps, not the loans, were put into a special-purpose vehicle—a kind of bank account held separately from their books, often in an offshore bank. JPMorgan paid insurance premiums into that vehicle. They tranched (sliced) that vehicle into securities and sold them to investors. Those investors, not JPMorgan, were on the hook for any defaults in the pool of three hundred loans (worth $9.7 billion) JPMorgan held. The first offering in December 1997 was called the Broad Indexed Secured Trust Offering (nicknamed "Bistro"). It was a stunning success. The tranches were gobbled up in two weeks by insurance companies and banks. Soon the method was copied throughout the financial industry.[1]

"Bistro" and credit default swaps solved the problem of having to assemble those time-consuming, cumbersome, and costly CDO pools composed of real mortgages. Why? Because a CDO made up solely of swaps can be created instantly. With the help of complex computer modeling, you could design the swap-insurance payments so they more or less mirrored a regular CDO pool of mortgages that already existed elsewhere. Your swap-enabled CDO (the synthetic CDO) would be sliced into tranches and would return the exact same income as a regular CDO that contained real subprime mortgages or other risky forms of debt. You've just doubled the number of securities without creating any new pools of mortgages.

This is the heart of fantasy finance. It's also the hardest part. So let's slow down and take this step by step.

Imagine that you're a banker and your bank already has a $200-million portfolio of subprime mortgages. You are worried that some of these risky mortgages might go under. You want protection. And you'd like to make some money through some fancy financial engineering along the way. Here's one way to do it. (To simplify things we'll put the wine glasses away and only create two tranches.)

> **Step one.** You set up a big bank account (your Special Purpose Vehicle) somewhere where the weather is warm, the beaches are nice, and there are no pesky regulations and taxes—like the Cayman Islands.
> **Step two.** You entice investors to put money into that account so that it equals the amount of protection you want on your subprime mortgages. In this case you'd

like investors to put $200 million into your beachside account. The rules that govern the account are: If any of your bank's subprime mortgages default, you are permitted to take money out of the account to cover those losses. The bank account is your insurance fund. You no longer have any risk to worry about.

Step three. Your only problem is to find a way to entice investors to put all that money into your account. Unless you're Bernie Madoff, you have to give them something real in return: money. So, you agree to pay a certain amount into that account every three months, just like you were paying insurance premiums. But of course you want to keep those premiums down. So you need to give your investors something else as well: various amounts of risk and various amounts of return. You give some of your investors *more* money if they are willing to gamble, and *less* money if they don't want to gamble. (You don't increase your overall premium payments. You just give out your total payments to your investors unequally.)

Step four: You give them various combinations of money and risk by setting up tranches. The investors in the top tranche are the *last* to lose their money in case you have to raid the kitty to cover your subprime mortgage losses. The bottom tranche investors are the *first* to lose their money if you have to confiscate it. To make that arrangement attractive you give the bottom-tranche investors proportionally *more* of your insurance payments so they get a very high rate of return. (You can afford to do so because there are only a few securities for sale in the bottom tranche.)

Step five: You temporarily invest the $200 million in the account in very, very safe treasury bills, bank notes, and money-market funds. This contributes to the interest payments that will go to the investors.

Step six: You then toast everyone involved, especially yourself. You have set up an account that is full of hard, cold cash (and very liquid, safe investments) held near a warm, sandy, unpatrolled beach. You and your bank can sleep soundly knowing that the money is all yours if you need it to cover losses should any of your mortgages default. You now have rock-solid investments on your books. In exchange, you have to put insurance premiums into that beachside account for your investors, but those premiums are much lower than the interest payments you are getting from your subprime loans. You're in the money and it's insured.

Now let's see why everyone involved likes this arrangement. The top-tranche investors are happy. They put money into your account and got a decent rate of return from your premiums. But they are the last to lose their money if you tap into the account to cover defaults. They sleep well because they have very little risk, but still a good return. In fact the rating agencies said this kind of top-tranche investment was AAA.

The bottom-tranche investors who put money into your account are happy too, but in a different way. They are happy like a gambler with an adrenalin rush—one who anticipates getting a big payoff at the gaming table. They know the money they invested could be lost to you should the housing market go sour, but they are getting a very high rate of return right now. They are betting that if the investment lasts long enough, they can get back much more than they invested, before something bad happens and you take some, or all, of their investment away.

And of course, you, the banker who dreamed it all up, get a very nice bonus. You get hefty fees from the money that goes into the account for putting the deal together, for setting up the account, for selling the investments, and for managing the whole shebang.

All of this happens without buying or selling any of the underlying

THE LOOTING OF AMERICA

mortgages. No time or money had to be spent assembling a new pool of mortgages. This is hall-of-fame financial engineering.

This was also the kind of "exotic and opaque" investment that was sold to the Wisconsin school districts. Without knowing it, the Wisconsin Five bought a tranche just one small step above the gambler's tranche. They didn't even get the upside of the gambler's payoff that should have come with it. (But they sure got the adrenalin rush when they started to lose.) They were putting money up to insure very risky debt held (or bet upon) by the Royal Bank of Canada (RBC). For accepting such risk, their rate of return should have been awesome—that's the upside. Instead the banks and investment brokers took very high fees and gave all the downside—the highest risks—to the school districts. As the default rate moved closer and closer to the school districts' tranche, the value of the schools' $200-million investment plummeted to next to nothing. Any day now, the default rate will hit the point that triggers the release of the $200 million to the Royal Bank of Canada. And since the school districts had borrowed $200 million to place that bet, they will still owe that too as well as the interest payments. They might have been better off investing with Bernie Madoff.

Now please hang on as we take one more bewildering step into fantasyland. In our example, we created a new security that insured a pool of debt your bank actually owned. But that's not entirely necessary. You could set up a synthetic CDO based on a pool of loans that *you didn't own at all*! You can go through all the steps outlined above *as if* you were insuring something real. But you, the derivative dealer or packager, don't need to actually own the underlying junk debt.

Say what? How can a banker or anyone else write a credit default swap on a mortgage they don't own? The answer blew my mind. Two parties can agree to write a swap on anything. Owning it is irrelevant, just like you don't have to own a real baseball team to play fantasy baseball. Unlike regular insurance policies that must conform to laws and regulations, you can use unregulated credit default swaps literally to bet on someone else's bonds or loans or mortgages or assets that neither you nor your betting partner (called your counterparty) own. It's as if a thousand people were allowed to buy fire insurance on your house. What's at stake is essentially a bet: Is the house going to burn down, or not? Is the bond going to go into default or not?

Since this is fantasy finance, let's pretend you are the Royal Bank of Canada. You could sell a synthetic CDO to the Wisconsin school system that was nothing but a series of bets on bonds or mortgages that neither the RCB nor the Wisconsin schools owned. You are literally placing a bet on something you can observe (the baseball game) but don't necessarily own (the real major league players). If the bond or mortgage you are referencing goes belly up, Wisconsin has to pay you. If the referenced assets do not default, you, the RCB, pays insurance premiums to Wisconsin.

Now let's get back to reality, which is stranger still. As of this writing, the lawyers for the Wisconsin Five still do not know what the school districts actually insured. They're not even sure if they insured something that the RCB owned, or whether they just were part of a bet in which neither the schools nor the RCB owned the bonds or debt that were insured. The entire $200 million may have been simply a bet on a pile of junk debt that neither party owned. And you wonder why the financial system collapsed?

One more time: You can make a wager on any asset that you can observe. You don't have to own it. As a result you can set up a giant set of tranched securities without owning the underlying assets. And you can sell those tranches to investors—and make fees from selling them. Welcome to the very heart of fantasy finance.

Fantasy baseball really does provide an apt analogy. The value of synthetic CDO tranches is based on the value of mortgages or credit card debt owned by someone else, just like the value of your fantasy baseball team is based on players under contract by the real major league teams. Fantasy baseball is a synthetic derivative that operates "on top" of real baseball. It has financial value because you're willing to bet on your fantasy baseball team, and everybody in your league is willing to bet on their own derivative teams and against yours.

Miraculously, synthetic CDOs are not limited by the supply of mortgages or bonds that are assembled within pools. One pool of actual subprime mortgages can prop up many sets of securities. First, you can set up a CDO that you tranche and sell to investors where you actually are selling real slices of those mortgages. Then you can set up multiple synthetic CDOs based on credit default swaps (insurance) on those tranches you already sold. This increases the number of securities that can be sold, based on the same set of mortgages. It also amplifies the fat fees for the creators and brokers. And it multiplies the risk to the financial system. If something goes wrong in the underlying pool of junk debt, multiple synthetic CDOs can simultaneously crash in value.

All of these synthetic CDOs are playing "on top" of those mortgage pools just like in fantasy baseball. In real baseball, all we have are the thirty teams in the American and National Leagues. But there are tens of thousands of synthetic fantasy baseball leagues that play using the statistics of the real major leagues. (Some estimate that right now there are fifteen million of us playing fantasy baseball.) So too in fantasy finance: There's no limit to the number of synthetic CDOs that can, in theory, be created . . . assuming there are those who are willing to pay premiums for the credit-default-swap insurance and those who are willing to buy the tranches formed around those premiums.

And it doesn't stop there. Credit-default-swap insurance also is a tool that can make high-risk equity tranches much more desirable. Toxic tranche buyers might want to hedge some of the risk they are taking on. Having too much of it on your balance sheet might make the credit rating agencies look askance. Credit default swaps allow you to remove the risk entirely (which is what the Royal Bank of Canada might have been doing with the Wisconsin school districts). During the housing boom, financial institutions (primarily investment banks and insurance companies) wrote swaps with the owners of equity tranches. For a period of let's say five years, the investment bank would insure the equity-tranche owner so that she would not lose her principal—in return for quarterly payments, just like an insurance policy. The equity tranche owner would continue to collect the high interest payments you'd expect from a risky investment, but in effect would share some of that risk and interest with the swap counterparty, which insured the principal.

In a very real way, credit default swaps enabled anyone to hedge their bets for any security at any time, in any place in the world. Anyone could unload some or all of their risk, or so it seemed. It worked beautifully—as long as everyone could pay their bets if the bonds or tranches ran into financial trouble. You can see why Greenspan admired the guile and genius of the derivative designers.

We now have the tools to explain how $300 billion of subprime and "Alt-A" loan losses could do so much damage. During the housing boom, synthetic CDOs greatly expanded the number of tranches that were sold all over the world. And credit default swaps increased the market for the toxic-waste tranches by insuring them. In fact, the subprime assets were referenced again and again in multiple synthetic CDOs. This more than *tripled* the $300 billion worth of subprime and Alt-A losses into a trillion dollars of losses on CDOs backed by risky housing debt. If we include the full range of CDOs backed by corporate, consumer, and housing debt, the estimated losses climb to about $1.6 trillion. Of that, our banks have suffered about $500 billion in losses on the CDO-type assets that they held on to. Combined with losses on more standard loans to corporations and consumers, the U.S. banking system has piled up about $1.7 to $1.8 trillion in losses, as of February 2009.[2] And that's just the banks. Other financial institutions, such as insurance companies, hedge funds, pension funds, and sovereign wealth funds, have been hit with similar losses. Financial engineering, like the sorcerer's apprentice, turned a bucket of polluted water into a toxic tidal wave.

Because this is so key, let's repeat it. Synthetic CDOs allowed the banks to sell layer after layer of securities based on the same underlying junk debt. Here's another analogy: They were able to sell the Brooklyn Bridge again and again (but that doesn't do justice to the bridge, which at least is solidly constructed). This process of selling multiple securities based on the same debt again and again turned a $300 billion subprime mortgage problem into a multitrillion-dollar fiasco.

While the subprime and junk-debt markets boomed, these banks and insurance companies were making enormous profits by selling and reselling securities based on the same risky debts. But the risk was amplified if something went wrong with the pool of subprime mortgages or bonds that ostensibly underlay all this betting.

Fantasy baseball fans will have an intuitive grasp of this danger. What happens to the tens of thousands of fantasy baseball leagues if the real major leagues go on strike?

———

This kind of fantasy finance would be relatively harmless if it was really like fantasy baseball—a form of gambling that doesn't change real baseball. Unfortunately, fantasy finance actually affects the underlying economy—even though neither the party who pays the premiums nor the counterparty who insures, owns the tangible asset that they're betting on. It's as if my fantasy baseball team could cause Yankee steroid star Alex Rodriquez (A-Rod) to have a good or bad year.

We can see some of the real-world consequences of credit default swaps by comparing them to home and life insurance. If you own your house, you usually take out fire insurance, just in case. And since you want to protect your family, you also are likely to purchase life insurance. Now imagine that someone you don't know also takes out fire and life insurance polices on you and your home. Why would they do that? You might start to worry that this mysterious insurance buyer was just waiting for your house to burn down with you in it. After all, they're paying good money for the chance to benefit from your misfortune.

Now imagine ten thousand people taking out fire and life insurance on you and your home. It would not come as a shock if someone tried to torch your house—after checking to make sure that you were at home. Or maybe these investors are just biding their time, essentially speculating that since you do seem to be getting on, you might just keel over before too long. So they bought the policy now while it's cheaper and hope to sell it later for a higher price if you're still alive by then. They're merely gambling on the odds of your survival. Small comfort.

Of course the regulated insurance industry knows that this would be bad for business. They understand that if ten thousand people take out fire insurance on your house, they will soon be asked to pay ten thousand claims because of a suspicious fire. So to get fire or life insurance, you have to have a material interest in the asset insured.

Not so with credit default swaps. You and I could get together to create an insurance swap on $10,000 worth of Corporate X bonds that neither of us own. You might be willing to insure those bonds if I gave you $1,000 up front and another $500 per quarter over the next five years. If Corporation X goes bankrupt or gets bought out or restructured (we must agree on the list of trigger events), you'd have to make sure I get the difference between $10,000 and what the bonds fetch after default. There are forms we can fill out that detail this bet—and a bet is exactly what it is since neither of us own any Corporation X bonds.

As of this writing there is an enormous swap market for this kind of corporate bond insurance. Trillions of dollars' worth of swaps are out on the bonds issued by developing nations and major corporations. Take General Motors: Some estimate that $1 trillion worth of GM swap bets are on the table right now.[3] (Other estimates are much lower, but no one knows for sure because the swaps are unregulated.) These are essentially bets about whether GM bonds will sink into default or swim. The vast majority of the swaps are among parties who don't even own GM bonds. They are just speculating on GM's demise. As of December 2008, GM was in such sorry shape that if you wanted to bet on the demise of $10 million worth of GM bonds over five years, you would have to pay your counterparty $8 million up front plus $500,000 per year.[4] Had you gotten into this action in 2005, your insurance swap would have cost only $304,000 up front and no yearly payments. That means your 2005 swap has greatly appreciated in value. You could now resell it for a sizable profit, assuming you could find a buyer. (In fact, these swap "spreads" are used by investors to gauge the risk of a company.)

Once credit default swaps are severed from real ownership of the underlying asset, the sky's the limit on what you can insure. For example, if you own shares of GM you might want insurance in the event that overall car sales go below a certain number per month. Enron, in fact, had a very profitable line of derivatives for agricultural firms and airlines that wanted to insure themselves against weather events. Some enterprising derivative dealer would be glad to help you find the perfect set of swaps to meet your appetite for hedging risk . . . and for outright gambling. And with each deal, the derivative dealers get a nice fee.

Right now the face value of all the swaps that exist around the globe is estimated at over $70 trillion—about four times the value of the entire U.S. economy. Some reports claim that's a vast underestimate—that the real number is more like $600 trillion. Others say it's "only" $50 trillion. In truth no one knows because the swaps are not regulated. In any event, it is certainly the largest casino game in human history.

Until very recently, Alan Greenspan believed this swap market was a most wholesome phenomenon because it dispersed risk.

He saw that all the sophisticated players could and did hedge their bets. He believed such swaps actually limited the economic damage caused when companies like Enron and WorldCom collapsed, because so many of the bondholders were made whole owing to their CDS-insurance protection. Greenspan believed these swaps limited the domino effect that such corporate implosions could cause.

But there are major systemic problems that the former Fed chairman chose to ignore. What happens when one of the big gamblers can't pay off its debts? Bear Stearns and Merrill Lynch were among the biggest bettors. By September 2008, the Fed realized that if either company folded, a run of credit default swaps would be triggered, and the two firms would be unable to cover the swaps they had written. If they couldn't pay, it could undermine a string of institutions that in turn might go bankrupt, triggering wave after wave of credit-default-swap payments and bankruptcies. Instead of allowing Bear Stearns to go bankrupt, the feds facilitated and guaranteed its merger into JP Morgan. Merrill Lynch was preemptively sold to Bank of America. Credit default swaps had connected these failing companies to thousands of critical nodes in the global financial system. (Since the bonds of these companies did not go into default, many of the insurance swap bets didn't have to be settled.)

We should be getting a sense of what was wrong with Greenspan's blind faith in unregulated markets—and with Congress's blind faith in Greenspan's "oracle" abilities. When the financial system was in decent shape, dispersing risk through unregulated default swaps seemed like a grand idea. The swaps seemed to create stability when a few corporations went under. But when the financial world experienced a more systemic problem—like the amplified collapse of the housing market—the credit default swaps started to turn toxic. Rather than dispersing risks, the swaps ended up twining them together, forming an intricate web that circled the globe. And so the collapse of even one large counterparty could bring down many corporations and cripple the world economy.

Nevertheless, Robert Pickel, head of the International Swaps and Derivatives Association (the trade group representing the major swap players), is in denial. As he told a Senate committee on October 14, 2008, "To say that [credit default swaps] were the cause, or even a large contributor, to that turmoil is inaccurate. . . . There is little dispute that ill advised mortgage lending, coupled with improperly understood securities backed by those loans, are the root cause of the present financial problems."[5]

Pickel is in a pickle. He, of all people, knows that synthetic collateralized debt obligations powered by credit default swaps drove the subprime housing market and enabled financial institutions to sell toxic waste securities all over the globe. He must know that credit default swaps created layer upon layer of leveraged securities based on high-risk mortgages and other debt. CDSs are at the heart of the casino, Pickel is representing the house, and we should not expect him to warn us about the dangers of gambling.

―――――――

If you feel things have gotten too technical, don't worry. We are returning to the fundamentals. To understand derivatives, we need to figure how money is made. Since it's all about money-making-money, let's look at how credit default swap sellers get rich.[6]

Let's say you're an enterprising derivatives trader at a big insurance company or investment bank. You learn that one of your clients is taking a $500-million bond position in Corporation X. You know they would like some protection in case Corporation X develops problems down the road. So, as an enterprising trader you offer to insure that very large investment through a credit default swap. In return for a ten-year guarantee, your firm will receive a fee of $12 million up front.[7] Nice work!

Wouldn't it be nice to book all of it as profit? Imagine your bonus. Unfortunately, even the most pliable accounting rules can't let you get away with that. Sure your firm can keep the money, but unfortunately it has to set aside some of the revenue to cover the risk. Needless to say, you, our enterprising derivatives dealer, want to set aside as little as possible. But there are a few rules of risk management that you must follow.

Here's a simplified model that you and your company might use to evaluate how much you have to set aside to cover risk. First you have to estimate how much the $500 million in Corporation X bonds would be worth if the company went bankrupt. The firm's financial statisticians check on the history of firms with ratings like Corporation X to determine that number. They discover that for a company like Corporation X, you are likely to reclaim about 50 cents on the dollar. So that means your firm actually is risking only $250 million (50 cents on every dollar of the $500-million investment). For profit-and-loss purposes, that should be the most your firm can lose for insuring Corporation X's bonds.

Next, we'll figure out a second risk that cuts in your favor: What's the likelihood that Corporation X will actually default in the next ten years? Your trusty financial number crunchers determine that only about four firms out of a hundred like Corporation X have defaulted over the last ten-year period—making for a 4 percent chance of default. That probability then gets turned into a dollar figure. So we multiply this risk by the amount of money at stake:

$$\$250,000,000 \times 4 \text{ percent} = \$10,000,000$$

Our statisticians and accountants now agree that it would be prudent to say that by insuring the original $500 million in bonds for ten years, the odds are you're on the hook for $10 million. So for accounting purposes, you must set aside $10 million of your $12 million in fees as reserves. The difference—$2 million—is your profit. Hallelujah!

But what's two million when you have to share it with your bosses? Can't we milk this baby for more? Sure we can. And it's not hard. To double our profit, all we need to do is tweak our risk assumptions just a little bit. Who among us wouldn't be tempted by such a prospect? After all, much of this is just guesswork. All we have are the odds.

Here's how we tweak. We have two risk numbers: how much we can get for the bonds during bankruptcy, and the chance of bankruptcy. We go back to our statisticians and we have them review it again. Lo and behold, with a little nudging from you (since they get bonuses too), they find that you can expect 55 cents on the dollar rather than only 50 cents. With this recalculation, we find that we're only risking a total of $225 million, not $250 million. We've knocked off $25 million in potential liability.

Next you take a more careful look at the default rate. You decide that the 4 percent was just a bit high, so you plug in 3.55 percent—because doesn't that seem just a bit more accurate? The stat guys say, "No problem, it could be 4, plus or minus a bit, so 3.55 percent looks okay to us."

You've made two very small changes and watch what happens:

$$\$225,000,000 \times 3.55 \text{ percent} = \text{about } \$8 \text{ million at risk}$$

You took in $12 million in fees. Your risk is estimated at $8 million. You now can book a $4-million profit instead of a $2-million profit. A little number jiggling and you've doubled your profit.

Imagine for a moment the incentives for such behavior. If you can jiggle, so can your competition. In fact, maybe you won't get the business at all unless you shave those points. Your whole job is at stake. As one CDO Web primer put it:

> Ah, competition! Competition is where the process starts to get interesting over time. Competition for credit derivatives business, for these easy profits, means that you and others in your company have powerful

personal incentives to make aggressive assumptions about how low credit losses will be, and to validate your co-workers' assumptions as well. If your assumptions are not aggressive enough, you don't win any business, you don't earn bonuses, your bosses don't earn bonuses, and you are quickly out of a job.

The institutional culture then very quickly becomes that if you want to keep your job—you and the other members of your group make aggressive assumptions. If you want to make big bonuses—you make very aggressive assumptions about how low the losses will be on the credit derivatives, which then translates into increased business for you. And yes, other people will need to sign off on your group's assumptions—but they are in the same institutional culture as you are, with their own personal reward systems that are based on the company making money. Also keep in mind that even the internal (theoretical) watchdogs are put in place by senior management, who have their own incentive structure, which is based on the company making lots and lots of money this year.

In a free market, where all the employees and senior management of all the financial firms want their piece of this lucrative action, the first thing that happens is that the firms with aggressive assumptions keep the firms with conservative assumptions from getting any business. And then, because we have competition going on here, in the next stage of the cycle, the very aggressive assumptions firms take the business from the merely aggressive assumptions firms. Then in the next cycle, the people making the very, VERY aggressive assumptions take the business away—and the bonuses away—from the merely very aggressive assumptions makers.[8]

Okay, Okay, we get it. To make higher profits and bonuses, these guys have to take on more and more risk. Why should we care?

We care because the more they cheat on their reserves, the greater the odds that they might default on their bets, which will lead others to default and so on until you've got the makings of a full-fledged disaster.

Think about it this way. Since there is no regulation at all, it is possible—even probable—that the financial company in the previous example that "earned" the $12-million fee will decide *not* to keep that $8 million in reserve at all. Why should they? They could invest that money elsewhere or loan it out. As a result, the institution may have no reserves at all behind the insurance they write and book. That makes the policy—the asset—practically worthless—an IOU without backing. If the economy is growing, no one cares too much. But what if the IOUs come due?

Here's a recent real-life example, the collapse of the banking system in Iceland, which had overextended itself all over the globe. The meltdown is awful for the Icelanders, but it's also a drag for the entire world financial system. Why? Because it turns out that Icelandic bonds are part of a great many synthetic CDOs. (That's because there are only about eight hundred corporations and countries whose bonds you can bet on. So the same bonds have to get used again and again.) According to Reuters, "Out of 3,771 synthetic CDOs rated by Standard & Poor's Corp. globally, 9 percent have one Icelandic bank name, another 9 percent have two and 14 percent have all three."[9] In other words, synthetic CDOs all around the world have insured the same Icelandic bonds, again and again. As these bonds go into default, the synthetic CDO tranches based on them will lose their value because they will have to pay up on their insurance claims. (How much they have to pay up depends on the value of the Icelandic bonds after bankruptcy.[10]) And we can be certain that the traders who created those synthetic CDOs also jiggled the odds in their computer models to minimize the risk, accelerating the crash in the value of all the tranches. The holders of those tranche securities will see their value plummet, which may put their own firms in financial danger, triggering yet another round of credit default swaps coming due . . . and so on.

Why should the dominos keep falling? The problem goes right back to those risk models. All of them were based on good-time assumptions—on the historical record of failures. But that record doesn't go all the way back to the Great Depression. Sometimes it doesn't go back any further than the go-go 1990s. The models didn't account for a major recession or a housing market collapse or any other catastrophic event. The jiggling all happened in the other direction.

Let's go back to our banker who trimmed down the odds. He got his bank to insure $500 million in Corporation X bonds, and used 55 cents on the dollar for what the bonds would likely be worth in bankruptcy. The chance of default was supposed to be 3.55 percent. Well, now the bonds are in bankruptcy. Had the analysts gone back further in time they might have used much higher odds, and therefore set aside larger reserves. Too late now. The bonds are in default. If those had been Lehman Brothers bonds, they only would be worth 8 cents on the dollar after default. That means the bank owes 92 cents on every dollar it insured for a total of $460 million out of the $500 million. But our banker had only taken in $12 million to insure those bonds (and $4 million was booked as profit and has long since vanished). His company is now out $452 million on the deal ($460 million minus $8 million in revenues after booking the profits). Ouch!

Firms everywhere were writing default swaps on each other thinking they were cleverly spreading the risk around. They thought they were laying off their bets (that is, selling the risk to others) and booking the profits. But by 2007, economic reality started to sink in. Nearly all the risk models turned out to be wrong. So instead of being on the hook for a few million dollars as the models predicted, they're actually expected to pay claims on firms like Lehman Brothers or Iceland or equity tranches that had gone belly-up. All of a sudden they're out billions: real money. All the big players in the credit-default-swap market—banks, insurance companies, hedge funds, large corporations—are looking at the possibility of huge losses now that they are being forced to align their models with reality.

Here is a chilling observation: It is possible that all the profits they booked and took home with them to their Caribbean retreats were phony. Those supposed profits have actually evaporated into billions of dollars in losses. Nine of the largest U.S. commercial banks have already seen their gains over the past three-and-a-half years disappear. On October 17, 2008, the *New York Times* reported that profits for these banks "from early 2004 until the middle of 2007 were a combined $305 billion. But since July 2007, those banks have marked down their valuations on loans and other assets by just over that amount."[11] A few weeks later, Fannie Mae reported losses greater than all its profits since 2002. So did AIG.

Let's pause to consider what those numbers imply. The nine largest banks pulled in $305 billion in *profit* over three and a half years. Fannie and AIG pulled in another $50 billion or so. Those profits paid for shareholder dividends, massive year-end bonuses for the elite traders and deal makers, enormous compensation packages for the top officers, and solid gold parachutes for the departing ones. Much of that money is no doubt tucked away in myriad assets, investment accounts, offshore tax havens, and the like. Yet all of the profits that luxuriously funded those compensation packages have vanished. You can take it to the bank that no one is going to voluntarily return his cut. Instead, you as the taxpayer are now shoveling those banks out of the hole.

And it gets more outrageous. Assume there's about $70 trillion of swaps out there and that a modest one-tenth of 1 percent fee was collected for writing them. That means the financial dealmakers may have already walked off with $70 billion in fees. That money is gone. What isn't gone is the $70-trillion liability. If more major companies default or are restructured, triggering the default provisions of the swaps, the collapse of the CDSs will deepen. And if the counterparties can't pay, there will be enormous pressure for Uncle Sam to come in. Yet again. Heaven help us if GM goes under and triggers a trillion dollars of credit default swaps.

As anyone without free-market blinders can see, you can't pin the derivative problem on Fannie, Freddie, or low-income marginal buyers. CDOs and CDSs were born and bred deep in the heart of our unregulated, free-market, over-the-counter derivative markets. These derivatives drove the market for subprime lending by turning junk mortgages into triple-A bonds, and they created a web of risk ensnaring the entire financial sector, and the rest of the economy along with it. These instruments are so complicated and opaque that no one but their creators can understand them (and maybe even they have not understood them thoroughly enough). Complex modeling and assumptions could be tweaked to fool rating agencies and investors. And the world was soon littered with toxic-waste securities that were supposed to be safe and sound . . . but are not, and never were.

We now have identified the largest components of the current crisis.

- *Collateralized debt obligations*, and their myriad tranches, made the sale of toxic mortgages respectable. They miraculously turned subprime mortgages into AAA-rated securities.
- *Credit default swaps* enabled the creation of thousands upon thousands of synthetic CDOs that were based on the same underlying pools of subprime mortgages (as well as other risky items, like credit card debt). This greatly multiplied the number of securities based on the underlying risky debt.
- Credit default swaps also *insured the riskiest toxic-waste tranches*, making them more attractive to investors.

- And finally, swaps linked together thousands of firms so that *a major failure of a few could paralyze the entire system.*

This helps us make sense of what the government was trying to do in the fall of 2008. The banks had a lot of toxic waste on their books—as well as hidden off their books through offshore special-purpose vehicles. At first, the government said it would dispose of that waste so the banks could stay solvent—that is, spend billions to buy it from them. Then it decided that wouldn't work, so instead they would inject large amounts of money into the teetering banks. The feds also had to protect large companies like AIG, Fannie, and Freddie, and merge away others like Bear Stearns and Merrill Lynch to keep the dominos from falling. Had the feds not intervened at all, it is likely that hundreds of banks and financial firms would have rapidly gone under. Then, we'd be staring straight into another Great Depression.

eight

Fantasy Finance Meets Reality:
The Great Crash of 2008

FOR DERIVATIVES TO BECOME "financial instruments of mass destruction," they needed an explosive trigger. And they got it with the bursting of the housing bubble.

There's a running argument about when the housing boom really started, why it grew, and what precisely caused it to crash. Some say it began after World War II when home ownership expanded rapidly. Others believe it started much later and was caused by easy-money policies on the part of the Fed and the Bush tax cuts. Still others claim it was a purely psychological phenomenon—bubble thinking—amplified by the media beginning in the early 2000s.

The evidence strongly suggests that mortgage-backed CDOs contributed mightily to the easy availability of mortgage money, especially for the riskiest homebuyers. We also know from previous financial bubbles that the financial casino always stokes booms. Even if you don't buy this idea, there's no question that housing prices shot through the roof during this decade. Chart 6 shows the most reputable housing-price index constructed by Karl Case and Robert J. Shiller, which shows housing prices shooting up "like a rocket taking off."[1]

During this period, housing prices accelerated much faster than the gross domestic product, which is not the typical pattern. From after World War II until 2000, the housing-price index and GDP trend lines ran almost perfectly in parallel. Not so after 2000.

The amount of money tied up in mortgages also skyrocketed, as seen in chart 7, provided by the Federal Reserve.

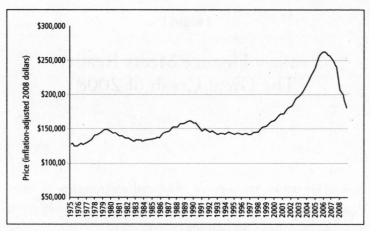

Chart 6. Real Median Home Prices in the United States. Case-Shiller Index, converted to dollar values, at http://mysite.verizon.net/vzeqrguz/housingbubble/.

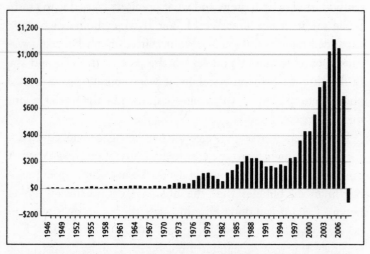

Chart 7. Total Value of New Mortgages Issued in the United States Each Year (in billions). Federal Reserve, "Flow of Funds Accounts of the United States," Federal Reserve Statistical Release Z.1, Historical data files, tables F.218, at www.federalreserve.gov/releases/z1/Current/data.htm.

As the boom took hold, more and more subprime borrowers were lured into the market. Mortgage brokers were hungry for the business because the fees were high. In November 2007, the Federal Reserve Bank of Dallas newsletter described the rise of marginal mortgages:

Some 80 percent of outstanding U.S. mortgages are prime, while 14 percent are subprime and 6 percent fall into the near-prime category. These numbers, however, mask the explosive growth of non-prime mortgages. Subprime and near-prime loans shot up from 9 percent of newly originated securitized mortgages in 2001 to 40 percent in 2006.[2]

The CDO fantasy-finance industry fueled that "explosive growth" through their magical alchemy of turning junk mortgages into AAA bonds. From the investor point of view, the risk of subprime mortgages virtually disappeared.

For a few years, it looked as if those holding these securities would make out like bandits because subprime defaults were actually *declining* as the boom accelerated. From 2002 to 2005 the share of subprime mortgages past due fell from 15 percent to 10 percent (see chart 8). As a result, equity-tranche holders might be clearing 20, 30, or even 40 percent returns. You can bet this accelerated the demand for more and more subprime mortgages to pool into CDOs.

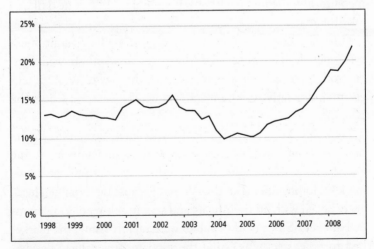

Chart 8. Subprime Loan Default Rates. Mortgage Bankers Association. The delinquencies are for mortgages that are 30, 60, and 90 days past due.

As the housing bubble swelled, speculators rushed in to buy up houses to flip—at the time of the bubble's peak, fully 20 percent of all home purchases were purely speculative[3]—profiting from the rising prices. Brokers peddled deceptive mortgage products to unsuspecting buyers. CDO salespeople pushed even the riskiest mortgage-backed securities onto pension funds and local governments that had no idea what they were buying. (To be sure some did know what they were doing and fell in love with the enormous projected returns.) The risk seemed to have evaporated, since home prices were going up and up.

"Get in now or you'll miss out on easy money," flashes the neon sign in front of the financial casino. "All winners, no losers."

Surely, our financial guardians saw this coming. Surely they were sounding the alarm. Not Ben Bernanke. However, he did address the subject as head of the Bush administration's Council of Economic Advisors in 2005, a time when housing values had lost any connection to reality. Bernanke acknowledged to members of Congress that home prices had risen by nearly 25 percent since 2003. But these increases, he said, "largely reflect strong economic fundamentals," including strong growth in jobs, incomes, and the number of new households.[4] I'll bet he'd like to take that back.

Then-Fed chairman Greenspan also refused to admit there was a bubble. He could allow that a few markets showed signs of "froth." But no one wanted to get in the way of Wall Street's gigantic derivative profit machine, which was propelling the boom.

There are many ways the Fed might have slowed down the housing boom—by tightening mortgage requirements at Fannie and Freddie, raising interest rates, or regulating derivative markets, for instance. But they didn't, because our financial leaders believed with all their heart and soul in self-regulating financial markets. Since market values were rapidly rising, the market had to be correctly assessing the fundamental values. Besides, they were dead certain that the financial system could handle a bust. After the dot.com bubble burst, the economy rocked a bit, but survived. Enron and WorldCom went belly-up, but the banking system stood firm. In fact, financial leaders believed that credit default swaps and other derivatives spread the risk of such busts and therefore protected the economy.

But this time the market miracle didn't materialize. At some point in all booms the gap between the bubble value and the real value gets too vast. And then reality breaks through. This time, the inevitable end came after homebuilders, reacting to rising prices, overbuilt. The supply of homes outstripped demand. There just weren't enough buyers left—subprime, speculators, or otherwise. The buying public was tapped out. They had too much debt, and their wages were stagnant (as we saw in chapter 2). And so, home prices declined. Meanwhile, reality slapped subprime borrowers in the face when their adjustable teaser rates shot up. More and more of these borrowers were unable to make their mortgage payments. If house prices had continued to soar, they could have refinanced at lower rates or sold their property to pay off their mortgages and maybe even have cleared a few bucks. But when prices sank, their homes were suddenly worth less than their mortgages: They were "under water." Behind in their payments and having no equity to protect, many borrowers walked away, leaving the keys behind.

You know the housing story from here. Prices plummeted as more and more defaulted homes came on the market. Entire neighborhoods suffered. Prime borrowers watched their home values deteriorate as foreclosed homes dotted their neighborhoods. Even Rust Belt cities that had missed the housing boom entirely saw their modest home values tank. Speculators with multiple homes were stuck. And developers with new projects could not find buyers. The housing casino was closing.

As people began defaulting on their subprime mortgages, risk magically returned to the tranches. The equity tranches, often held by banks, large financial institutions, and pension funds, were the first to go belly-up. Then, as defaults rose past historical levels, the mezzanine tranches also failed. Soon the supposedly secure AAA tranches started to absorb losses. Even if the defaults didn't go all the way to the senior tranches, the protective cushion below them was gone—and so they no longer merited their high credit ratings. Their prices crashed. In a flash, the emperor had no clothes.

For every "real" subprime tranche that went under, many synthetic tranches built from swaps on those mortgage pools crashed as well. It was as if the major leagues went on strike and destroyed thousands of fantasy baseball leagues.

Credit rating agencies were soon on the hot seat. They had received millions upon millions in fees from financial institutions to rate CDOs. Inevitably they blessed the senior tranches with AAA ratings, and the world's investment community relied on those ratings. Triple-A CDOs littered the globe. To produce those ratings, Moody's, Standard and Poor's, and Fitch's relied on models developed by the very firms that wanted the high ratings.

In theory, models for pricing and rating CDOs and swaps are designed to account for risk based on the probabilities of an uncertain future. Before computers this was nearly impossible to do. How do you figure out the risk of a mortgage pool with a thousand subprime mortgages from a variety of housing markets? What assumptions do you make about the default rates and the recovery rate in foreclosure? Tough stuff.

It got a little easier in 1972, when computers first entered the picture (even if getting access to one meant punching cards and standing in line at your university's one mainframe). Fisher Black, Myron Scholes, and Robert Merton developed a model to price options. (Scholes and Merton later got the Nobel Prize for it.) Their model gave people who were buying and selling futures and options a good idea how to price them. Within two decades mathematicians had figured out how to model CDOs as well. Many of the models were proprietary, owned by the very firms that were seeking the ratings. It was extremely hard for the ratings agencies to second-guess these high-powered mathematical constructs. (Also, there was money to be made by not second-guessing the models. More on that in chapter 9.)

Again there is a fantasy baseball echo. When the first American League–based fantasy baseball league in the country started in 1981 (the American Dream League[5]), we had no idea what we were doing. We'd conduct auctions for players, assemble our teams, make trades, and do the statistics by hand. Within a few years, one of our fantasy-team owners, Alex Patton, noticed that every year Eddie Murray, the Orioles slugger, went for $40 in our draft. (In our league each team had $260 to pay for a team of fourteen hitters and nine pitchers.) Each year our auction "market" felt like it could count on Steady Eddie to hit .300 or better, club 35 or more home runs, and drive in over 100 runs.

Patton astutely observed that if those stats were worth $40, then he could price every other hitter in our auction based on his estimate of what each player was likely to accomplish during the upcoming year. With those relative prices in hand he became the best bidder and clobbered us all for several years running. So even in the derivative dreamworld of fantasy baseball, models are extremely valuable. In fact, several of us got into the act and published our numbers in books and magazines. Twenty-five years later Patton is still at it, and runs a profitable online service with Peter Kreutzer that prices players. He awaits his Nobel Prize for fantasy baseball.

In fantasy baseball, nothing terrible happens if your model turns out to be flawed. People will stop buying your books or using your Web sites. Plus, you'll drop rank in your fantasy league and be humiliated in front of your peers. There's always next year. Our faulty models have no impact on real baseball. But as we are learning painfully, when fantasy-finance models go wrong they can cripple the real economy.

I don't have the mathematical skills to dissect financial derivative models. But our Princeton statistics professors did impart to us one extremely valuable concept: "Garbage in, garbage out." No matter how elegant your model, no matter how sophisticated your mathematical tools, if your initial assumptions are wrong, your results will be wrong, perhaps disastrously so.

It seems fairly certain that the CDO models bankers used to rate their tranches were based on several faulty assumptions. The first was that the low default rates for subprime borrowers we saw during the bubble would continue to remain low. It's as if flood insurers failed to account for 100-year floods. If the models had assumed a higher rate of defaults, then the CDO tranches might not have seemed so golden. But of course the pressure was on to ignore more dire assumptions. (To be sure, a few astute traders took the other side of these bets and profited enormously when the market crashed. But most followed the models into the abyss.)

In making their models, traders also made assumptions about what the "recovery rate" would be—that is, how much a house whose owner had defaulted would resell for. During a period of high appreciation the recovery rate would be very high. One would expect to get back almost the full value of the mortgage if the home had to be sold after default. Of course there were carrying costs, but these could be estimated and modeled in. However, rapidly declining housing prices could—and did—decimate the resale price of homes in default—as well as tranches based on more rosy recovery rates.

The quants also made assumptions involving something called "correlation." Their models assumed that the behavior of each mortgage or bond in the underlying portfolio pool was independent of the other—that the impact of one bad event was unconnected—"uncorrelated"—to another. For example, if a subprime borrower went belly-up in Las Vegas, the models assumed that this event would be unconnected to a default in Miami. Further, a slew of defaults in Las Vegas would not affect the overall market for homes, and declining housing values in general would not cause resale prices of defaulted homes to slide.

But when the bubble burst, the entire market turned out to be correlated. The defaults *were* connected, as were housing values. The models had been disastrously wrong.

———

Frank Partnoy and David A. Skeel, Jr., described these pitfalls in their prescient 2006 paper, "The Promise and Perils of Credit Derivatives." As they put it,

> The process of rating CDOs becomes a mathematical game that smart bankers know they can win. A person who understands the details of the model can tweak the inputs, assumptions and underlying assets to produce a CDO that appears to add value, even though it really does not. The mathematical precision of the models is illusory. . . .[6]

The authors took their analysis one step further. After looking carefully at how CDOs worked, they expressed strong doubts that it was possible to turn a financial sow's ear into a silk purse. How did CDOs actually produce value? Where did the high fees "earned" by the derivative dealers come from? The authors arrived at two polar-opposite possibilities. One was that the CDO creators had found an amazing, previously overlooked, inefficiency in the bond and mortgage markets: Somehow pools of junk bonds and mortgages had been vastly underpriced, and the tranching process had uncovered and released this hidden value. In that case, CDOs created value by solving a "substantial and pervasive market imperfection." But the authors were skeptical about this theory, which, if true, would represent "the most substantial inefficiency ever found in the finance literature."

And then we have the other possibility, which they found far more credible: The CDO industry actually created no real value at all. And more disturbing still, rather than solving a market imperfection, the CDOs "are being used to create one."

Danger ahead.

Partnoy and Skeel's most worrisome line is worth repeating: "A person who understands the details of the model can tweak the inputs, assumptions and underlying assets to produce a CDO that appears to add value, even though it really does not."

As we've seen, much money was to be made by slightly jiggling the assumptions. It appears to have netted the traders billions and billions in fees. The competitive pressures in the derivative market for CDOs practically guaranteed such jiggling. But the scariest part of Partnoy and Skeel's statement was that CDOs were not merely useless, but actually introduced *negative value* into the financial system. If they were right, those triple-A rated CDO tranches were, in fact, junk.

And they were right. A couple of years after they sounded their warning (only to be ignored by the Greenspans and Bernankes of the world), reality hit and the market for buying and selling CDOs dried up. And understandably, no one any longer trusted the models to determine the risk of these securities. The ratings agencies, of course, had egg on their face. They looked like money-hungry fools. They quickly reclassified triple-A CDOs to the junk bond status from which they came.

Suddenly, all manner of pension funds, insurance companies, university endowments, banks, and local governments saw their secure triple-A bonds turn to junk. They had to dump them, or at least try to. But there were no takers. The price for these investments was now a complete mystery since the market for buying them had dried up. Some might be entirely worthless, but there was no way to be sure. If you owned a CDO squared, you could be pretty sure you had piles of junk. If you owned a synthetic CDO based on swaps on high-risk equity tranches, you were screwed. As a result of the crash in value, the private over-the-counter market for these securities shut down. You were stuck with your toxic waste. (This is what they mean by "illiquid markets.")

Some investors were stuck in a living hell, like Karen Margrethe Kuvaas, mayor of Narvik, Norway, high above the Arctic Circle. To boost the town's revenues, she had heeded a trusted Norwegian brokerage house, which suggested she invest the town's funds in AAA-rated mortgage-backed CDOs. She was told that these securities were safe and would provide a better return for the town than government bonds. The extra revenue would support the town's schools and generous social services. But after the housing boom went bust in the United States, the value of Narvik's investments fell by $64 million through the end of 2007. Suddenly the town was facing a 40 percent budget cut. They couldn't make payroll. As the *New York Times* reported, "'I think about it every minute,' Ms. Kuvaas, 60, said in an interview, her manner polite but harried. 'Because of this, we can't focus on things that matter, like schools or care for the elderly.'"[7]

Had the financial toxic waste only polluted towns like Narvik, the crisis could have been contained easily. But it poisoned major financial institutions as well.

If you're a bank or an investment house holding billions of dollars of these securities and/or swaps on them, you're in big trouble. Some of your assets, maybe most of them, just evaporated. You've got to write them down and you've got to raise more capital. You might also have to sell other assets to stay solvent. The more you sell, and the more the others sell, the more steeply the prices drop. Your liabilities might be greater than your assets because the value of a whole bunch of housing-based securities just vanished. Your books are full of toxic waste. You're teetering on bankruptcy.

And it gets worse.

———

It gets worse because of the swap part of the financial equation. Many of the major CDO players also were major swap players. They had made bets all over the place. If one of the major swap players—like Bear Stearns, for example—goes under, billions of dollars' worth of swaps also go under. Bear Stearns won't be able to pay out on the swaps it wrote. Those who wrote swaps on Bear Stearns's debt also would have to pay up. It didn't take long for the CDO toxic waste that polluted Narvik to contaminate Bear Stearns, Merrill Lynch, AIG, Fannie Mae, Freddie Mac, Wachovia, IndyMac, and Washington Mutual, forcing the government to merge them away or take them over. Lehman Brothers also went down but was not rescued.

Here's how CDOs and CDSs collapsed AIG, the largest insurance company in the world. AIG, once a highly profitable company, had earned a triple-A rating on its debt. In addition to its renowned insurance and leasing divisions, it had gotten into writing credit default swaps because—well, they were just too sweet to resist. AIG wrote book on (that is, issued unregulated "insurance" on) more than $450 billion in swaps on all kinds of securities, including the most risky equity tranches. The company used its AAA status to make those it insured feel safe and sound. Also, because of that rating, they didn't have to put up any collateral for the insurance they wrote. They just collected the premiums. It was like minting money. The holders of these tranches paid AIG up front and then made periodic payments to be insured against the possibility that their CDO securities would default. In effect, AIG was getting hundreds of millions in fees just for a promise. But these deals were based on the assumption that AIG would keep its AAA status. The swaps stipulated that if AIG's ratings were lowered, the company would have to put up collateral to make sure they could pay off the bets. AIG thought the odds that the triple-A-rated CDOs they were insuring would default were minimal—and the odds that AIG itself would be downgraded were positively minuscule. AIG felt secure and rich. Partridge hunting anyone?

Now watch what happens when those triple-A CDOs turn to toxic waste. As we've seen, when the housing bubble burst and subprime mortgage defaults multiplied, the rating agencies often reclassified the tranches as junk—and many tranches went into default.

AIG now had to pay up to those it had insured against default. But in making good on those IOUs, AIG ran out of cash. They tried to raise billions in a hurry, but lenders refused. Not only did lenders in the private markets recognize that it would now be risky to give money to AIG, but a lot of these lenders were in a similar pickle with CDOs and swaps themselves. When the credit agencies saw AIG starting to struggle, they lowered the ratings on AIG debt—which triggered the collateral requirements of the swaps. Now AIG needed massive infusions of cash or it would go under. It tried to sell assets but it was too little, too late. To prevent collapse and utter chaos, the feds stepped in with about $100 billion and in effect took over the teetering insurance giant. (The cost of that bailout jumped to about $180 billion as of March 2009. At that time, AIG was posting a loss of $60 billion and in negotiations for more federal money.)

In addition, the Federal Reserve Bank of New York set up a new entity, Maiden Lane III, to buy up and remove synthetic CDOs from AIG books. The idea was to have Maiden Lane III purchase the underlying assets and unwind the swaps so that AIG could be relieved of the burden. Then if the underlying assets somehow grew in value again, Maiden Lane III, which is jointly owned by the New York Fed and by AIG, would reap the gains. In the spirit of fairness, one would hope that the Federal Reserve or the U.S. Treasury also would buy up the synthetic collateralized debt obligations that were foisted onto the Wisconsin school districts. (As of this writing, such a request is being made by the Kenosha Teachers Association to the Wisconsin congressional delegation and to the Fed.)

Had AIG gone bankrupt and failed to pay up on its swaps, company after company that relied on that money might have failed as well. This would have triggered more swap payments and more failures, with no end in sight. It could have been the equivalent of the bank runs that led to the Great Depression.

Joseph Cassano, who ran the small unit of AIG traders in London responsible for this fiasco, was confident this scheme would work. As late as August 2007 he told investors that "It's hard for us with, and without being flippant, to even see a scenario within any kind of realm of reason that would see us losing $1 in any of those transactions."[8] When it came to his own money, that, indeed, was the case: His compensation totaled $280 million over eight years and earned him a million a month for six months as a "consultant," after he was forced to retire in April 2008.

To add insult to injury, in March 2009, AIG, which by then was eighty percent owned by the government, used taxpayer money to pay out $165 million in bonuses. Many of the bonuses went to those in the division that cooked up the disastrous derivative insurance that drove the company and the economy into the ground. Edward Liddy, AIG's chief executive, then came up with one of the lamest excuses since "the dog ate my homework." He wrote to treasury secretary Tim Geithner, "We cannot attract and retain the best and the brightest talent to lead and staff the A.I.G. businesses—which are now being operated principally on behalf of American taxpayers—if employees believe their compensation is subject to continued and arbitrary adjustment by the U.S. Treasury."[9]

Frank Partnoy, like virtually every financial writer, deploys a gambling metaphor to explain how the few major derivative dealers could bring down the house. He writes, "Imagine a poker game where everyone is borrowing from everyone else. Now supposing the biggest loser goes bust after losing a big bet with someone not at the poker table. Suddenly, all of the poker players at the table are insolvent."[10]

But let's take that metaphor a step further. Imagine that each insolvent player is now unable to pay his debts to players at other poker tables. Those other poker tables would go bust as well, and so on, right through the casino. Or, in reality, right through the entire credit system.

Enter the famous "credit freeze" of 2008. What exactly is that? In chapter 2 we used the analogy that the banking system in general provides the oxygen for the real economy. Like the air we breathe, money flows in myriad directions at the same time.

Companies use short-term loans on a daily basis to cover expenses like payroll. They need longer-term loans to invest in their plants, equipment, and research and development. Mortgages, car loans, student loans, credit cards, all need bank funds to circulate. Even the Wisconsin school districts borrow short-term money each year to smooth out their income flows as they wait for local tax revenues and state funds to arrive.

But this circulation depends on basic bank-to-bank loans. Smaller banks in the hinterland lend their surplus deposits to big banks in the financial capitals who in turn lend the money to large employers back in the hinterland. Large banks lend back and forth among each other for countless purposes. If they stop, all manner of lending grinds to a halt. And grind to a halt it did, once those derivatives went bust.

Think about it from the point of view of one of the nine surviving large national banks. You've got billions of dollars' worth of CDO assets that have plummeted in value. You are afraid to sell them because then you'd have to book the enormous losses and you might be declared insolvent. So you hold onto them and pray they come up in value. You also have billions upon billions of dollars' worth of swaps that might soon come due if other banks and companies fail. In fact you have bets in all directions—you're giving out insurance and buying insurance. Because of the crash in your toxic assets, you might have to write them down, so now your capital base is declining. You need more capital. You're also worried about having enough cash around to meet any unexpected obligations from the swaps. And to top it all off, you know for dead certain that every other financial institution is in a similar fix. Even if you thought you could profit by making loans to other banks you hold back because you don't know how bad off they really are since their toxic assets are hidden in special-purpose vehicles.

Given these conditions, are you going to lend away your precious money? No way. You'll sit tight, thank you very much.

And that's exactly what banks did (and are still doing as of this writing). They don't trust anyone and for good reason: They know they are loaded with toxic waste and they know everyone else is as well. If they lend, they might not get paid back. It's taken massive federal guarantees to start unfreezing some of these markets. So far, all the government has managed to do is turn some of the ice to slush. We're still a long way from freely circulating financial air.

With inadequate financial air, it's just a matter of time before the "real" economy asphyxiates. No car loans mean very few car sales. No mortgage money means sharp declines in home sales and prices. Workers get laid off. Consumers stop spending. And the economy spirals downward.

Ben Bernanke, the self-proclaimed Great Depression "buff," did not take these events lightly. In a flash, his academic research no longer was academic. He knew full well what could happen if the financial system froze up and lending ceased. It happened in the 1930s, and now it was happening again.

Bernanke attacked the crisis the way his research suggested it should be attacked. Recall that he subscribed to Milton Friedman's view of what caused the Great Depression. He thought economic research had proven that speculative booms did not have to lead to disaster, even when they burst. While the 1929 stock market crash certainly caused a major disruption in the financial system, it did not have to lead inevitably to the Great Depression. Instead, Bernanke believed that the Federal Reserve had failed to provide enough liquidity to keep the economy going. It failed to bail out enough banks and inject enough money into the banking system to break the freeze. And the Fed of the 1930s had stayed glued to the gold standard, which actually reduced the amount of money circulating around the globe. In Bernanke's view, economists had conclusively demonstrated that countries that had avoided such tight-money policies during the 1930s had ducked the worst of the Depression.

So as the financial crisis deepened, Bernanke knew just what to do. He lowered the Fed interest rates to just about zero. And he sounded the alarm. He knew that if the financial atmosphere stayed depleted for any length of time, the economy would slide into recession, or worse. It had to. There just would not be enough credit available for business as usual. More and more businesses would fail. And since so many institutions were linked together by swaps, the failure could spread rapidly around the globe. Bad news.

Bernanke also avoided the worst of free-market ideology. He, treasury secretary Henry Paulson, and other top Bush administration officials could not look the other way and pretend that the financial free markets would resurrect themselves. That would guarantee the next Great Depression. Government had to intervene and intervene directly.

Bernanke soon realized that the intervention would have to be massive. First the Fed helped to merge Bear Stearns into JPMorgan and to guarantee about $25 billion in toxic waste stuck on their books. Then they took over Fannie and Freddie, and guaranteed more than $200 billion in junk securities held by the two. They let Lehman Brothers fold. But they had to loan over $100 billion to AIG, which held nearly a half trillion dollars in credit default swaps. They helped to merge away Merrill Lynch and Washington Mutual—companies that had been badly burned at the CDO casino. Next they asked for $700 billion from Congress, ostensibly to clean the banks' books by buying up as much financial toxic waste as possible.

When all of that didn't work fast enough, Bernanke basically proposed nationalizing the nine major banks (without calling it that), as Sweden had done in a previous crisis and England was doing in this one. He and Paulson chose a very mild form of temporary nationalization: They gave the banks a massive injection of capital in return for preferred shares. The government also received stock warrants that give it the right to buy shares of the banks in the future for a price set now. If the banks increased in value, taxpayers would be rewarded through these warrants. But, they didn't want to interfere too much with bank operations, so the government set no conditions on how the money could be used. After all, they all were bankers and shared an understanding about how the game should be played.

Had Bernanke become a socialist? Hardly. Fundamentally, he didn't trust the very government he was part of. As he put it during questioning before the House Financial Services Committee on February 25, 2009, he wanted to rely on "private sector specialists, not government bureaucrats."[11]

But he was not about to go down as a dumb free-market ideologue. He was clearly coming to terms with the obvious fact—the financial free-markets had run amok. Only massive government interventions, here and abroad, could save our financial system from crashing and taking the real economy down with it. The Fed had failed in 1929. This time Bernanke would get it right.

If the Bernanke-Friedman theory of the Depression is correct, these massive "loans" to the financial sector will get the economy moving again. More capital from the Treasury will make the banks solvent and will renew lending. Step by step, the Fed will be able to unfreeze the various financial markets, from corporate money markets to student-loan securitizations. We'll have a recession, maybe even a deep one, but nothing more chronic.

But what if the current crisis isn't really about a bank capital shortage? What if the crisis stems from larger, structural problems? What if these guys are wrong about the Great Depression? Maybe conservative scholars *haven't* really disproved the liberal-left theory of the Depression. Maybe it actually *was* a crisis of overproduction and underconsumption caused by the decline of working-class buying power during the late 1920s. Maybe our current crisis really happened because most of the productivity increases that should have gone to increase workers' wages instead went to "the investor class," and then into the fantasy-finance casino. And maybe the trigger was that consumers couldn't keep piling on more debt to buy goods and services since their real wages had stalled over the past twenty years. What if the Bernanke-Friedman theory is just plain wrong?

We're the guinea pigs and we're in the process of finding out.

nine

The End of Fantasy Finance?

You want fantasy finance? Turn on cable financial news and you can still find free-market cheerleaders tossing their pom-poms high in the air.

Rah-rah: Government interference has distorted free markets! Freddie Mac and Fannie Mae have propelled the nation into the subprime crisis by giving mortgages to unworthy lower-income people.

Sis-boom-bah: Government regulations blessed the three rating agencies and allowed them to mislabel securities, which exacerbated the subprime crisis. And the bailouts and stimulus plans will make it all worse.

Go-Markets-Go: Remove any and all government constraints, lower taxes and let the wisdom of the markets work its magic!

Even as the entire credit system freezes solid, throwing the global economy into crisis, former senator Phil Gramm sings the fight song. As he recently put it, "By and large, credit-default swaps have distributed the risks. They didn't create it. The only reason people have focused on them is that some politicians don't know a credit-default swap from a turnip."[1]

Fortunately, no serious policy maker, vegan or otherwise, is listening. Most realize that market fundamentalism is no match for the real world. They know that defusing the crisis will take a hefty dose of government intervention. One would hope that the era of blind faith in financial markets is over. Fantasy finance has hit reality and we're done with delusions.

Or not.

Even some moderate pundits are warning of "too much government interference" in the financial sector. Thomas Friedman, for example, writing in the *New York Times* on October 26, 2008, argues that government intrusion could prevent banks from taking the kind of healthy risks needed to "grow the economy." Now that the government has become the largest investor in the nine major U.S. banks, Friedman thinks we should give the banks a little privacy. He asks us to imagine a couple of young, hip entrepreneurs, like the two who founded Google, walking into a bank that is under government supervision and asking for a loan. Friedman suspects that the banker would say, "'Boys, this is very interesting. But I have the U.S. Treasury as my biggest shareholder today, and if you think I'm going to put money into something called 'Google' . . . you're fresh outta luck."[2]

Oh, you know what staid government bureaucrats are like. They are too thick and cautious to see what Friedman calls, "the fine line between risk-taking and recklessness. Risk-taking drives innovation; recklessness drives over a cliff." He wants someone or something to curb the recklessness without killing the risk taking.

Sound familiar? This argument goes all the way back to the financial bubbles that roiled England in the early nineteenth century. Then, as now, economic liberals tried to navigate the fine line between risk taking and recklessness, between innovative finance and the casino. They never found that line. Instead, they repeatedly let the casino run wild. And, with the partial exception of the Great Depression, after every bubble and inevitable bust, the business class managed to resist regulation. Even then they avoided the strongest regulations proposed by advocates like Keynes, and after a few short decades managed to weaken and dismantle even those that had been imposed. Today, we will fail yet again, as long as thoughtful opinion makers and policy setters conflate real-world economic investment with fantasy finance.

I doubt Ben Bernanke or other policy makers are particularly worried about banks loaning money to funky start-ups. Starting the new Google would require a tiny sum compared to the trillions of dollars that at the moment are frozen in the financial markets. The real problem is what to do with those dangerous derivatives. Lending to the next Googles had stalled well before the government started its interventions. Banks stopped lending because their balance sheets were polluted with toxic-waste derivatives, and they were teetering on the edge. So now the government is infusing them with public funds and government guarantees so that they will start lending again. It's the banks that now are risk averse, not the government.

Thomas Friedman also warns us that regulation is no substitute for good management. He argues that banks like JPMorgan Chase and Banco Santander in Spain "are not surviving because they were better regulated than banks across the street, but because they were better run. Their leaders were more vigilant about their risk exposure than any regulator required them to be."[3]

That's a very low bar to clear. The most risky derivatives that turned into toxic waste are still completely unregulated! We should not forget that JPMorgan Chase was up to its eyeballs in many questionable derivative deals that helped Enron cook its books. And right now, JPMorgan Chase is part of the problem: They're contributing to the credit freeze the government is trying to break. They're certainly not loaning much out to young Google-like entrepreneurs. And investors and shareholders might welcome significantly more regulation on the "vigilant" leaders of Banco Santander who lost over $3 billion to Bernie Madoff's Ponzi scheme.

It's risky business singling out exemplary banks. They all played in the casino and any one of them, at any moment, could go down. Perhaps it's time to move beyond regulatory phobias as well as risk-taking fictions. It's increasingly clear that without the firm hand of the government, we're toast.

———

Most financial leaders agree that we must create wise regulations to control these financial excesses. The consensus seems to be that we need more "transparency." When world policy leaders from Ben Bernanke to Nicolas Sarkozy wring their hands about "exotic and opaque" derivatives that are too complex to understand, they conjure up the casino's back room—the place with the lap dancing and other illicit activities. When they tell us we need "transparency" within the credit default swap and CDO markets, it's as if they want to shine a bright light into that dim room, hoping to halt the unsavory transactions. Will that work or will the fantasy finance just find another dusky room to do its business?

In 2003, Frank Partnoy, a noted expert in the field, proposed a thorough set of reforms. He focused on credit default swaps and CDOs, and was particularly exercised by the potential damage from synthetic CDOs. Like us, he was awed that these items involved swaps on bonds neither party owns. He called them "the ultimate in financial alchemy."[4]

Partnoy knew that CDOs could not miraculously increase the value of the portfolio of bonds or mortgages from which they were derived. The tranche slices could not really be made more valuable than the underlying pool of assets. And yet, he noticed, the increased value enabled the derivative dealers to siphon off about 2 percent of the total cost of the tranche in fees. Plus, investors got higher rates of return than comparably rated investments. (Gunter Meissner in his textbook, *Credit Derivatives*, claims that the fees were more like 10 percent.) How could they pull that off?

Partnoy believed the fictitious increase in value came from gaming the credit agencies—the oligopoly of Standard and Poor's, Moody's, and Fitch's that put their seal of approval on the tranches. These agencies were granted unique status by the Securities and Exchange Commission, which has enabled them to become highly profitable gatekeepers for the investor community. Based on the ratings they assign, these agencies can either permit or prohibit a financial institution from buying a certain security. Under federal regulations, a top rating opens large markets among banks, insurance companies, pension funds, and the like.

How did the derivative dealers receive such favorable ratings?

Here is Partnoy's complaint. (I couldn't resist.) He argues that derivative dealers at the major commercial and investment banks hoodwinked the poor schmos at the rating agencies.[5] Partnoy does not mince words:

> Anyone looking closely at the credit-rating agencies would find it difficult to justify their importance. The analysts at the three rating agencies were perfectly nice people, but they were not—to put it charitably— the sharpest tools in the shed. Banks snapped up the best analysts, and investment banks hired the second best. Based on their recent track record, the remaining employees would have done a better job if they had simply followed the business section of a daily newspaper.[6]

And this was written in 2003, long before our current meltdown, but after the collapse of Enron, Global Crossing, WorldCom, and Orange County, whose debts were vastly overrated by the credit agencies to the bitter end.

Synthetic CDOs are incredibly complex to analyze because their value depends on a vast array of underlying bonds or mortgages. It takes intricate (error-prone) modeling and incredible skill to get even an approximate estimate of their true risk. As we've discussed, the models were manipulated. Partnoy reports that bank employees privately admitted to him that "they could tweak these models to make a CDO deal appear to add value."[7]

So, what if a ratings-agency employee detected these shenanigans? That was easy to solve, said Partnoy: "the banks doing the CDO deal would hire him or her, at a significantly higher salary."[8]

Partnoy's complaint has since been studied by academics and validated. In their paper for the National Bureau of Economic

Research released in January 2009, Professors Thomas Philippos and Ariell Reshe concluded:

> In retrospect, it is clear that regulators did not have the human capital to keep up with the financial industry, and to understand it well enough to be able to exert effective regulation. Given the wage premia that we document, it was impossible for regulators to attract and retain highly-skilled financial workers, because they could not compete with private sector wages.[9]

This problem worsened after 2003. That's when the credit rating agencies began to realize that they could reap huge profits by giving triple-A ratings to these exotic instruments. It was big business. From 2002 to 2007, their revenues doubled from $3 billion to $6 billion. Moody's profits quadrupled between 2000 and 2007, and it had the highest profit margin of any company in the S&P 500 for five years running.[10]

The pressure was on to rate anything and everything as favorably as possible, lest the competition land the deal. After the bust, congressional hearings revealed the inevitable embarrassing e-mail and instant-message traffic within the ratings agencies: "We rate every deal," wrote one ratings agency analyst to another. "It could be structured by cows and we would rate it."[11]

(Wisconsin, no stranger to cows, became a victim of these bogus ratings. The school districts were told that they were investing in double-A securities, when in fact they were getting securities that should have been rated like junk bonds.)

To help their bank clients achieve the highest ratings for their CDOs, the ratings agencies actually helped the derivative dealers adjust the tranche structures. The agencies also tested the tranches using a mathematical technique called "Monte Carlo." According to a July 2007 report, "The Ratings Charade" in *Bloomberg Markets Magazine*, the Monte Carlo program "effectively rolls the dice more than 100,000 times by running the information randomly."[12] Supposedly this technique helps to determine the default probabilities of CDO tranches. However, as one ratings executive put it, "If the input data that you use is a little bit uncertain, your numbers are going to be trash, but they will look convincing."[13]

With the world looking for targets, the credit rating agencies are now in the crosshairs. Members of Congress complain that their constituents who trusted AAA ratings feel betrayed. They are angry and want heads to roll. Even Alan Greenspan is tossing them under the bus, saying, "The consequent surge in global demand for U.S. subprime securities by banks, hedge, and pension funds supported by unrealistically positive rating designations by credit agencies was, in my judgment, the core of the problem."[14]

Who knows what will happen to these benighted credit agencies. Obama officials are discussing ways to have them financed from sources other than from the companies they are supposed to rate. Some free marketeers believe the only solution is to open a flourishing market for more and better credit agencies, free of "government interference." But the odds are that the derivative dealers would quickly learn how to game these new agencies against each other until they got what they wanted.

Partnoy has suggested that we could rein in the ratings agencies by removing their "free speech" defense in lawsuits. As things now stand, the credit agencies are considered to be offering "opinions" and so cannot be sued for just being wrong. For the time being, the agencies are coated in cow dung and will probably exercise extreme caution in doling out high ratings. And Congress will be keeping them under a very bright light until the crisis lifts.

What to do about "exotic and opaque" derivatives is a tougher problem. The consensus is that it's past time to adopt the regulatory proposals offered more than a decade ago by Brooksley Born and the GAO. We should stop allowing investors to trade unregulated derivatives in that dark back room. All deals should be recorded properly on the balance sheet, including over-the-counter trades. Prices for all derivatives should be available online to everyone. Once we all can see them, the worst abuses should stop. Investors will run from companies that rely on exotic and opaque derivatives.

The standard wisdom is that simply by regulating all securities and derivatives, we will remove much of their raison d'être—to skirt regulations that govern other securities. When banks wanted more leverage than they were permitted under banking regulations, they used derivatives. When private firms like Enron wanted to show a steady rise in profits, they used mysterious swap derivatives (offered by Thomas Friedman's good managers of JPMorgan Chase). Few major firms could resist the temptation of using the unregulated derivatives to manipulate what they had to disclose. As Partnoy put it, "As long as 'securities' were regulated, but similar 'derivatives' were not, derivatives would be the dark place where regulated parties did their dirty deeds."[15]

Partnoy and others also are calling for stiffer criminal prosecutions against lawbreakers. Many on Main Street would love to see a few billionaires share a cell with Bernie Madoff.

Will these new approaches solve the problem?

I have my doubts. Even the most astute critics are continually dazzled and blinded by financial engineering. For example, in his 2003 book *Infectious Greed*, Partnoy actually *praises* both the derivatives and the banks that use them. He writes, "Derivatives and financial innovation generated great benefits, enabling parties to reduce risks and costs." Even more surprising, in describing the collapse of Enron, WorldCom, and more than a hundred other companies in the early 2000s, he writes: "The regulators, too, have remained composed, in part because banks, which now use credit derivatives to reduce their risks, have virtually *eliminated the threat of a system-wide banking collapse*, the primary concern of regulators in the United States" (emphasis added).[16]

That passage, from one of the most astute derivatives critics, is worrisome. How could he get it so wrong? As we have learned painfully, the "threat of system-wide collapse" was not eliminated. It happened—credit derivatives helped *make* it happen.

One conclusion we must draw is that the derivatives in question are much more lethal than Partnoy suspected at the time—so lethal that "transparency" might not be enough to make them safe.

Why did critics like Partnoy, as well as the establishment leaders like Greenspan, so underrate the danger of derivatives? Why didn't they sense the threat to the financial system as had the GAO and Born a decade earlier?

Perhaps they were fooled by past experience. They'd seen that the collapse of nearly a hundred corporations earlier this decade did not harm the banking system as a whole. There was no system financial meltdown during the post-9/11 economic slow-down and stock market drop. The apparent conclusion was that since the banks were major players in derivatives, they must have hedged themselves very well, that they had identified the risk and dispersed it. In fact Partnoy worried that they were dispersing the risk to others who were far less equipped to handle it. But even under duress, the essential features of our credit system remained intact.

"Infectious greed" (the infamous Greenspan phrase Partnoy used as the title of his book) probably helps explain why knowledgeable people failed to sound the alarm about derivatives. Partnoy hints at this when describing how American Express lost $826 million on corporate bond CDOs in 2001. Starting in 1997, American Express, a highly sophisticated financial operation, created pools of corporate bonds and sliced them into tranches. It kept the safer, low-risk, super-senior slices for itself and sold the higher-risk tranches to adventuresome investors. After Long-Term Capital Management crashed in 1998, AmEx couldn't find buyers for the riskier tranches. This was the obvious time to stop creating CDOs. But the fees were so good that AmEx continued to tranche away.

So what did AmEx do with those unsellable risky tranches? It held onto them! When several corporations in the underlying pools defaulted on their bonds, the lower tranches crashed in value. The losses in the pool were so great they pulled down the value of the higher tranches as well. Quicker than you can say "fantasy finance," AmEx was out nearly a billion dollars and its chairman, Kenneth Chenault, had to admit publicly that American Express "did not comprehend the risk."[17]

Partnoy and Greenspan believed that after this 2001 debacle, no one would be so stupid again—certainly not the major banks and investment houses, who always hired the best and the brightest. Obviously, the banks that created the equity tranches knew they were toxic waste that needed to be disposed of. Partnoy was certain that the big derivative players would use credit default swaps to unload the risk onto other investors like a "hot potato."

Greenspan claims to be stunned that so many institutions kept toxic waste on their books, and admits he should have accepted more regulation. As he put it on October 23, 2008, "Those of us who have looked to the self-interest of lending institutions to protect shareholder's equity (myself especially) are in a state of shocked disbelief."[18]

But even after AmEx, the major banks repeated the same mistake: They kept the toxic-waste tranches when they couldn't sell them, because they just wouldn't let go of the fees on the entire CDO. They were too delectable, and the returns on the equity tranche were enormous . . . while they lasted. Even a keen student of greed or bubble psychology could not imagine that AIG would book billions of dollars' worth of bets to insure CDO subprime tranches, and then not hedge their bets. Partnoy and Greenspan were sure that credit default swaps would disperse risk. They never imagined that the banks that were at the heart of the credit-default-swap business would crash the entire financial system.

Greenspan the defender and Partnoy the hardcore critic both got it wrong. And if so, how can we expect even the most astute knowledgeable regulator to get it right?

The fundamental flaw is that nearly all the reformers assume that credit default swaps and CDOs have intrinsic economic and social value. They assume that we can use these instruments to disperse risk efficiently, lower overall credit costs, allocate credit more efficiently, and protect the credit system as a whole. It seems the major piece of evidence for this position is that the financial markets placed value on CDOs and swaps, and by assumption, market value means economic worth. Yet Partnoy himself in 2003 and again in 2006 suggests that CDOs are fool's gold—that the only value they have comes from gaming the credit agencies and avoiding regulations. As the government tries to figure out how to pluck toxic CDOs from polluted bank balance sheets, can we still say they have "real" positive economic value?[19] After all, there is no market for these instruments unless the government steps in to create one with massive loans and virtual profit guarantees. Much of their value seems to have evaporated into the recesses of fantasy finance. I'm waiting for someone to admit to the possibility that these bold new financial "innovations" were never socially useful in the first place.

The bottom line is that *there is no evidence that credit default swaps have helped stabilize the financial system.* All of the evidence points to the exact opposite conclusion. If AIG had been allowed to succumb to market forces and go bankrupt, the financial dominos still would be falling all around the globe.

It's high time for the defenders of collateralized debt obligations and credit default swaps to show us the money, not just in theory but in tangible gains for the real economy. Where is the evidence to justify their worth?

The decision makers who once charged that the regulations proposed by Born and the GAO would cool the "cauldron of financial innovation" are now pushing for those regulations themselves. But they still cling to the old language, warning that we must be sure not to kill creative genius—that financial innovation must be encouraged and not stifled through regulatory reform.

Maybe we need some financial Luddites to step forward. It seems pretty clear that "financial innovation" ran amok, creating more financial toxic waste than we can handle. If financial innovation leads us into economic catastrophe, we should at least consider what the world might be like without so much of it. Maybe the casino already has enough games of chance to last a millennium.

And finally, there's Partnoy's complaint. How can we develop an effective regulatory régime governing these complex derivatives when the sharpest "tools in the shed" have already been bought off by the banks? How will the government find and retain competent regulators when they can be so easily lured away?

It's a case of simple economics. You'd have to be a powerfully self-possessed, civic-minded person to work for the government when you could be earning 10 to 100 times more at a bank, investment house, or hedge fund. If you're smart enough to understand the myriad complex derivatives, then odds are you won't be working for the feds for long. (Unless maybe you're Henry Paulson or Robert Rubin or Rahm Emmanuel, and you've already made your millions on Wall Street and can afford a stint of public service.) Imagine the temptation for a young government regulator who is smart enough to master derivatives. How long would it be before the fast-spinning revolving door whisks her away toward a seven-figure salary?

Perhaps the Obama administration's call for public service will draw forth idealistic experts that comprehend these "exotic and opaque instruments." But it would be a lot easier if we narrowed the enormous compensation gap between the financial industry and every other sector in the economy. (We'll return to this problem in chapter 11.)

———

Not only does the financial sector make money from money, it also mints new money. When we put one hundred dollars in a commercial bank, regulations allow the bank to make a series of new loans totaling approximately $1,150.[20] Quite literally, the bank is creating new money through those loans by leveraging your deposits. When investment banks and hedge funds leverage 30, 50, or even 100 times their base capital, they are creating wads of new money. The unregulated derivative markets created huge amounts of leverage. Just think how much money people made from synthetic CDOs and CDO-squareds, all based on a relatively small number of real underlying mortgages. As asset prices rose during Greenspan's term at the Fed, so did the ability of derivative dealers to further leverage those increases. CDOs and credit default swaps in combination and separately helped stir up the froth of fantasy finance.

Let's slow down and walk through this idea of leverage. Anyone who has a mortgage is using leverage. If we put 20 percent down and borrow 80 percent, our leverage is 4 to 1 (debt to equity). With that leverage we can make a very nice return from our investment. For example, if the price of our home increased by 20 percent, our equity would increase by 100 percent. Of course, leveraging also means we could lose more. If our home's value declines by 20 percent, our equity is wiped out.

Financial derivatives increase leverage. Options allow you to use a relatively small amount of money to buy a claim on a large amount of stocks, bonds, or commodities. When you think about it, credit default swaps also enhance leverage. If you are insuring a bond and receiving payments, you've created a new security out of nothing. You've put up nothing but are receiving payments. You can then use your new asset—the swap—to borrow more funds. And when you have insured an asset through a swap, you've made that first asset more valuable and should be able to leverage more loans on it.

Regulated banks used off-the-books special-purpose vehicles to create and hold CDOs. Those CDOs allowed banks to increase their leverage beyond the regulatory limits. In fact, our global casino never runs out of ways to make sure its patrons enjoy the benefits of leveraging.

Can there ever be too much leverage?

We said that "real" economic production takes place on the

surface of the earth. And we said that finance is the atmosphere—the clouds and the air that allow our "real" earthly economic entities to breathe and grow. This financial atmosphere is directly connected to "real" production, because all loans are claims on the "real" assets of the global economy. A certain, but unknown, amount of financial air is needed for robust economic production. Too much can lead to violent economic storms. "Fantasy finance" is the drifty, opaque stuff building up in the atmosphere.

This simple image allows us to pose fundamental questions: What is the proper balance between the financial air and the "real" economy on the surface of the globe?

Here are some scary statistics provided by Charles R. Morris in *The Trillion Dollar Meltdown*. "Not long ago, the sum of all financial assets—stocks, bonds, loans, mortgages, and the like, which are claims on the real things—were about equal to global GDP. Now they are approaching four times global GDP. Financial derivatives, a form of claim upon financial assets, now have the notional [face] values of more than ten times global GDP."[21]

While one may quibble with Morris's numbers, he is describing layers of financial atmosphere floating on top of the "real thing." Some of these layers help the "real" economy below breathe and prosper. But too many layers are a problem, since each layer of leverage makes claims on the real economy. While most commentators in 2007 thought the economy could easily weather the housing downturn, Morris predicted that we'd lose at least one trillion dollars' worth of financial value. He underestimated by several trillion . . . and counting.

So: How do we reduce the extra fantasy-finance layers before they destroy us?

First we need to take a closer look at what kind of capital makes up the financial atmosphere. Some of those extra "fantasy finance" clouds may be pumped up there by clever derivative dealers, but they're there for a reason. Derivatives are created to solve problems for investors (for a fee, of course). Sometimes derivatives help investors get around tax laws and other kinds of regulations. Other times they enable a firm (like Enron or WorldCom) to post fictitious revenues. Most often, however, they are designed to generate higher returns for investors and fatter fees for the derivative dealers.

And those fantasy-finance clouds actually come from somewhere, even though they've been hugely puffed up by fancy financial engineering. What is the primary source of that capital? Left-leaning as well as mainstream economists seem to agree that our current fantasy-finance clouds were inflated by surplus global capital searching for higher returns.

But where did all that surplus capital come from? This is key to understanding our crisis and takes us back to where we started in chapter 2. As the economy was deregulated starting in the mid-1970s and then accelerated by Reagan's tax cuts and further cuts in regulations, wealth shifted to the very richest among us. The weakening of labor law and the attacks on unions made it increasingly difficult for working people to bargain for their fair share of rising productivity. These trends were reinforced when the Soviet Union collapsed and capitalist globalization took hold. The fall of the Iron Curtain opened up new markets and gave global producers access to cheap labor. The emerging economies of China and India also provided cheaper labor and vast new markets. The growing global labor markets put downward pressure on U.S. wages, while productivity and profits rose rapidly. The world became awash with profits. Because the supply of surplus capital was so high, the rates of return in sound financial instruments were relatively low. Those holding the global surplus capital were eager to find good investments. But they were running out of "real" economy investments that matched the level of risk they would accept.

In our metaphor, they couldn't find high enough returns on their investments on the surface of our economic globe. The clouds of fantasy finance provided a new attractive home . . . for a while. CDOs in their various shapes and sizes were sold as sure things, and they were gobbled up by all manner of institutions and investors from all over the world. Credit default swaps were sold to further protect investors who owned the shakier tranches. All this created more and more layers of leveraged finance— more and more fantasy-finance clouds puffed up with capital that couldn't find enough sound investments back on terra firma.

As we saw in chapter 2, the real wages of U.S. workers stagnated and declined starting in the mid-1970s. Yet productivity continued to rise. For the first time, there was a growing disconnect between those two trends. Not only were American workers forced to compete with cheaper labor from around the world, but fewer than ever were in unions. Profits increased, and the investor class got enormously wealthy. Tax cuts moved even more money to the top. Meanwhile, workers went deeper in debt to maintain their consumption levels.

Who funded that consumer debt? Much of it came from fantasy finance. The surplus capital captured by the investor class from around the world bought into new securities made deceptively safe and attractive by complex derivatives. In effect, some of this surplus capital had been recycled, via CDOs, into risky mortgages and consumer debt. But it turned out that the risk had not been engineered away.

Our current crisis, therefore, is not really about a housing bubble here or a dot.com bubble there. It's about a long-term fantasy-finance bubble—too many clouds of surplus capital and derivative-created leverage. If this is correct (and even mega-investor George Soros seems to agree[22]), long-term reforms must keep the fantasy-finance clouds from expanding. We need to control the financial community's ability to create more and more leverage—more and more financial atmospheres that inevitably become unstable and threaten the real economy below. Even more importantly, *we need to find ways to bring that surplus capital back to planet earth.*

How do we reduce those extra cloud layers of fantasy finance? Regulations would certainly help as they did during the Depression and from then through the collapse of Bretton Woods. But in our incredibly complex global economy, we also need additional tools to prevent the creation of fantasy-finance bubbles.

Here's our framework: First, move money from Wall Street's paper economy to productive real-economy investments (chapter 10); and second, move wealth from the top of the income distribution back to the middle and the bottom (chapter 11)— precisely the opposite of what we've been doing for the past three decades.

ten

Proposals Wall Street Won't Like

HISTORY IS A CRUEL TEACHER, especially when we're hard of hearing. The Mesopotamians carefully regulated money-making-money to avoid social chaos. Jewish law mandated periodic debt forgiveness (the "Jubilee Year") for a reason. The Koran and the Catholic Church forbade usury to prevent financial enslavement. Even if you don't buy Marx's dire predictions, our many booms and busts might make you wary of unrestrained financial markets. The Great Depression painfully forced us to rein in high finance. But by 1980, greed-driven amnesia had set in, and the elites in our society embarked on another disastrous experiment in deregulation. Now, yet again, money-making-money has brought us to our knees. The gods worshiped by our ancestors must be having a good chuckle.

History also has taught us that finance is not just another sector of the economy. It ties all sectors together. It also functions like a casino, only the bets are placed with other people's money—so the inevitable meltdowns destroy other people's lives. The largest financial institutions are considered to be too big and too central to fail. Because of their wealth and structural position in the economy, they exert enormous power over public policy. President Clinton was only half kidding when he noted the possible connection between his reelection and a "bunch of fucking bond traders."

This is not a bankers' conspiracy. It's structural. As long as financial institutions are permitted to move vast sums of wealth around the globe at will, those markets will dominate the economy. As long as financial compensation reaches into the multimillions and even billions of dollars, the rules of the financial casino will be written by Wall Street. And as long as we fuse necessary economic financial functions and the speculative casino, the financial system will, sooner or later, melt down.

Unless your name is Rip Van Winkle, you have noticed that in the fall of 2008 the federal government "loaned" the financial community more than $1 trillion. (Some say that by February 2009, the total hit $2 trillion when you include Fannie, Freddie, AIG, the Bear Stearns merger, and Citigroup. And if the Obama Administration removes toxic assets from the banks, the price tag could hit $3 or $4 trillion.) Why such largesse? Because the economy collapsed when major financial institutions approached insolvency and stopped lending money to each other and to everyone else. This happened because the unregulated financial instruments these institutions had created, and profited wildly by, turned out to be toxic waste, with little current market value.

Please step back to take a cold, hard look. At least a trillion dollars was handed to big bankers in 2008 and 2009, with very little debate. This is borrowed money that we, the taxpayers and our children, are on the hook for. It's an immediate transfer of wealth from present and future generations to the largest financial institutions in the world. It may well be the largest wealth transfer since African Americans built the South. We went along because the financial markets had a gun to our heads. No bailout, no lending. No lending, no economy.

Maybe someday we'll get it back. Maybe we won't. If we're lucky, the capital infusion will prevent another Great Depression, and we hope that's worth the cost. And maybe one day we might even make a little extra from the bank stock warrants the government now owns. All of this, however, is pure speculation. As usual, we're rolling the dice.

If you're looking for a sure bet, here's one: Working people will suffer because of the reckless deployment of Wall Street–created derivatives. Even if the $787-billion stimulus package passed in February 2009 works extremely well, millions of working people will suffer long periods of job loss and face declining state and local services.

There's nothing speculative about the collateral damage from the fantasy-finance meltdown. By March 2009, the unemployment rate had jumped to 8.5 percent. More than 690,000 additional workers lost their jobs that month—the worst single month in thirty-seven years. The combined 3.3 million job loss for the five previous months is the worst since 1945. More than 5.3 million jobs were lost over the previous year. The Bureau of Labor Statistics also compiles the "jobless rate" (called U-6) by adding together unemployed people who are actively seeking work, people who aren't actively looking but don't have a job and say they want one, and people who are employed part-time because they couldn't find full-time work. The jobless rate for March 2009 was 15.6 percent—more than 23 million people! And still climbing rapidly.

State budgets are withering all over the country. The Center on Budget and Policy Priorities estimates that forty-seven state budgets will be in the red by a total of more than $350 billion through 2011.[1] For example, in Alabama, state tax receipts are crashing, leading to cuts in public education. As one school official put it, "We're having programs cut, purchases of textbooks deferred, class sizes increased, programs like art, music and physical education cut, even more than in the last few years."[2] Superintendents have been told to let leaky roofs go on leaking. The children in those dilapidated classrooms—and millions more across the country—are paying for the financial toxic waste, right now.

And yet, some people are talking about the need for "shared sacrifice." You see, "we" have lived beyond our means. From the greedy executive, to the greedy credit card debtor, to the greedy subprime borrower, to the greedy child in a school that expects a roof that doesn't leak, we're all to blame. We used our home equity line as a private ATM. We went into hock to buy a car and a flat-screen TV. It's time we tightened our belts . . . *after* we've given a trillion dollars to the financial sector.

David Brooks, the *New York Times* columnist, writes that we are entering an era of scarcity "in which smart young liberals meet a stone-cold scarcity that they do not seem to recognize or have a plan for"[3] . . . *after* we've given a trillion dollars to the financial sector.

Nearly every Republican in Congress is attacking the Obama administration for wasteful social spending. They say we no longer can afford costly liberal dreams of student scholarships or massive investments in infrastructure and green technology. We've got to scale back our expectations . . . *after* we've given a trillion dollars to the financial sector.

But to fix the economy, are we supposed to rein in our spending or do we need to spend more to stimulate economic activity? John Maynard Keynes called this the "paradox of thrift." If we save more and spend less (which is what we started to do by early 2009), aggregate demand in the economy as a whole goes down, and we push the economy further and further into recession. While it makes sense for each of us as individuals to pay off our debts, if we collectively do so during this decline, we exacerbate the decline. As a result, Keynes argued, the government must step in to boost the aggregate demand—there's simply no one else to do it.

The Obama administration has pressed ahead with a $787-billion stimulus program to try to reignite the collapsing economy. It is acutely aware that if we're going to learn from the Depression we should get the lesson straight. After the New Deal programs enacted in his first term had begun to bear fruit, Roosevelt restrained federal spending during his second term in the name of fiscal probity. And in doing so, he dumped the economy into a second major depression in 1937–38. It took the massive expenditures of World War II to finally get us out. The New Deal did not, as conservatives argue, go too far. It didn't go far enough. And the current trillion-dollar bank bailout and stimulus package might not go far enough either.

Now that the U.S. Treasury vault has been smashed open, what should Main Street demand? The Obama administration is counting on a stimulus program combined with more support for the banks and housing to "create or save" 3.5 million jobs. This is further supported by an ambitious budget plan to increase investments in energy, education, and health care. It will certainly put in place an array of new financial regulations. It will try to bring transparency to the derivatives market through open trading on regulated exchanges. It will bring hedge funds under regulatory control. It will control mortgage companies that encouraged lax lending standards. It is even asking for certain limits on executive salaries at institutions that receive federal largesse. Also it is pressing to reform the rating agencies so that they might truly act independently of those they are supposed to evaluate.

All of these reforms would surely help. But the lessons of history show they will not provide us with sufficient protection from the casino. The financial industry is likely to resurrect itself and again dominate our economy. Financial institutions will remain too big and too important to fail.

We need to go beyond regulations to divert fantasy finance toward human needs—toward real investments in infrastructure, in renewable energy, in science, in health care, and in education.

The financial world has grown immeasurably more complicated than during the New Deal. It would be sheer hubris to claim that we understand the vast chains of financial ties that crisscross the world. Their size, speed, and complexity will make it extremely difficult (maybe impossible) to predict how regulatory reform will play out. No one really knows for sure how to prevent people from exploiting loopholes to create new financial casinos where they can again gamble with our resources. As long as the financial incentive is there, bright and clever financial innovators will find ways to speculate. They are likely to invent new financial products, undercutting the best intentions of the rule makers.

Besides, regulatory reform addresses a symptom but not one of the major root causes of the problem. Financial derivatives could not work their magic were it not for surplus capital looking for investment opportunities. Unless we redirect that capital, we will never be able to rein in the fantasy-finance casino.

So what can we possibly do when faced with such vast uncertainties? For starters, we can take a page from the financial sector: We can hedge. We should develop a rock-solid insurance policy to protect us from fantasy finance and its propensity to create financial crises.

Extraordinary times call for extraordinary measures. The bankers and industrial giants have figured out bold survival strategies for themselves. Raid the vault! We should do the same. To be sure, the public coffers also should be opened to fund robust public investments. *But instead of just raiding only our own treasury, we should raid the fantasy-finance vault.* We need a piece of the casino's action, starting now.

Financial Disaster Insurance

We need protection from the big boys. We need a collective insurance policy against meltdown. Therefore, we, the taxpayers as represented by our government, should collect insurance premiums from every nook and cranny of the financial sector, beginning immediately. The premiums would pay us back both for the current raid on the treasury and for the recession created by fantasy finance. The premiums also would help indemnify us for the next financial tsunami. Unless we entirely eliminate private financial markets, we can expect a never-ending chain of booms and busts. Yes, we should mitigate them through wise regulations and consumer protections. But no one can assure us that we'll never see another bust. Therefore *we should demand insurance premiums against the probability of future financial meltdowns*—collective protection against the worst-case scenario. We need our own credit default swap on the entire financial sector.

The best way into the casino vault is to hit up all financial transactions. How much casino action are we talking about? According to historian Niall Ferguson, "Every day two trillion dollars change hands on foreign exchange markets. Every month seven trillion dollars change hands on global stock markets." He also calculates there are about $3 trillion in CDOs out there and that the estimated value of credit default swaps "was just under $600 trillion."[4] By my back-of-the-envelope calculations, I estimate that the global casino sees about $900 trillion worth of transactions each year, plus or minus a few hundred trillion. If we collected a 3-basis point insurance premium (three one-hundredths of 1 percent or less than 1/3 of a penny per dollar) on the face value of each and every transaction, we could collect about $2.7 trillion per year in total global premiums. I suspect the U.S. share would be at least $500 billion per year, year in and year out.[5] Of course, we would have to be careful not to exempt any kind of transaction: It would only invite our financial wizards to build new instruments based on the exempted activity.

You want to speculate against currencies? You want to dive in and out of the markets every few nanoseconds? You want to buy and sell credit default swaps and CDOs? Go to it. But on each transaction you've got to pay an insurance premium to the public. Why? Because history has taught us that at some point the activity you are engaging in will contribute to the next financial sector bust, and we'll have to suffer the damage and clean up the mess.

But won't this encourage even more of a moral hazard, since the financial community would know a bailout would be coming? First, these funds should *not* be designated for bailouts. They should be used to help us rebuild the economy after financial turmoil. When I say we need "financial disaster insurance," I don't mean that this is insurance the financial industry pays to protect itself. I mean insurance that protects us *from* the financial industry, paid for by the industry since it is the source of potential harm. This is like medical malpractice insurance. Doctors and hospitals pay for malpractice insurance to cover the cost to a patient if they have caused that patient harm.

Because of the critical role of the financial sector, when it malfunctions the entire economy suffers. We need income to help us survive the economic crashes since no one yet has figured out how to have private capital markets and *not* to have booms and busts.

But will this fund eliminate the need for bailouts of failed banks and systemically important financial institutions? No, but it might reduce their frequency by draining excess capital from financial markets and moving it into the real economy. We can't promise, nor can anyone else, that after this crisis, public money won't again be used to save the financial system. But in the meantime, under our financial disaster insurance plan, we'd be getting revenue to build a stronger real economy.

But shouldn't the fees depend on the instrument and its level of risk? No. Such micromanaging is asking for trouble. It would be hard to determine the risk profiles and it would be even harder to figure out how to translate them into a fee structure. But more importantly, such differentiation would be red meat for the derivative industry. Inventive quants and lawyers would certainly work long, hard hours to devise new instruments that avoided the higher fees and qualified for the lower ones.

In the United States, I would urge that the insurance premiums—the $500 billion or so each year—go directly to repair Main Street: for renewable energy, infrastructure, health care, and education—the most vital real investments a society can make. Again, we are not calling for the fund to be set aside to bail out the financial industry. Instead we're asking that the fund prop up the real economy that will, sooner or later, suffer, as we are suffering now, from collapsing financial markets. Again, we are draining money from the fantasy-finance casino and moving it toward the real economy.

But isn't financial disaster insurance really a tax? It's both. It is a tax because it moves money from the private financial sector to the public's coffers, as all taxes do. It is insurance because, acting collectively through our government, we are trying to insure ourselves from the economic damage done when the financial sector gets into serious trouble, which it is prone to do with great regularity. We need the tax/insurance because *no one* can possibly assure us that our current disaster will end anytime soon, or that another one won't befall us in the next decade or two. No one can provide us with real collateral to back up the claim that regulation will prevent the next meltdown. At this point in human history, we'd be very naïve to believe that we can prevent free-market bubbles through regulations or more consumer protections and support. To ignore our boom-and-bust history is to engage in another round of bubble thinking, of irrational exuberance, of faith-based economics. Regulations will always be imperfect. And financial wizards are notoriously ingenious when there are billions of chips on the table. With financial-disaster insurance, they'll have to slide some chips our way each and every time they spin the wheel. The insurance premiums/tax should be viewed as the price financial institutions must pay for free financial markets, above and beyond income taxes, which all of us should pay as citizens.

Is this practical? Won't financial markets, which are electronic, just move to areas with no insurance premiums? This is a vexing problem that will require a great deal of diplomacy to solve. But it should be worth the effort. This proposal works best if the world's economic powers—offshore islands as well—join in a global insurance program. Financial markets connect us all. The tsunamis are truly global. And every nation has an interest in insuring itself from fantasy finance.

The core of this idea is not original. James Tobin (1918–2002), a Nobel laureate and Yale economist, proposed a global tax of 1 percent on the transfer of currencies between countries. He believed that this tax (which became known as the Tobin tax) would limit currency speculation, which can destabilize the financial system and several times has caused extreme hardship in developing nations. He also hoped funds collected through the tax would be used to eradicate poverty.

An outrageous proposal? A year ago, maybe. But outrageous is the new commonplace. Who would have expected a $1-trillion bailout of financial institutions? Who could have predicted that the ultra-free-market Bush administration would have essentially nationalized key banks and insurance companies? Financial chaos has cracked open the door of the financial casino. Outrageous is in, perhaps including the idea of having financial polluters pay to clean up their toxic wasteland.

———

We are in the middle of the largest bailout in history. "Innovative" financial instruments with questionable social utility have imperiled banks and corporations around the globe. These financial products have polluted the global financial system, putting the underlying economy at risk. CDOs and credit default swaps have wrought destruction in communities that invested in them— from Narvik, Norway, to Whitefish Bay, Wisconsin. If the companies in question had sold deadly prescription drugs instead of toxic financial instruments, we would expect the authorities to shut them down. Certainly, we would expect the government to develop strict controls for drug approval *before* such products could ever again be foisted on the populace.

But when it comes to financial-product safety, we let the market police itself. Apparently, Alan Greenspan honestly believed that it was in the self-interest of financial entities to contain their risk—or else investors would lose confidence. He was wrong and now admits it. The major derivative dealers were in a mad race to pump out more and more toxic products because the fees they yielded were staggering—a veritable fantasy-finance gold rush.

Milton Friedman didn't believe the government should regulate any product, including drugs, whether legal or illegal. The Food and Drug Administration, he once said, "has done enormous harm to the health of the American public by greatly increasing the costs of pharmaceutical research, thereby reducing the supply of new and effective drugs, and by delaying the approval of such drugs as survive the tortuous FDA process."[6]

Most of us, however, know that we need the government to protect us from dangerous products rushed to market by profit-hungry food and drug companies. In today's world, it is simply impossible for individuals to research and verify all the claims that salesmen make. Is this actually a chemotherapy drug that will help cure me of cancer, or toxic waste repackaged in an IV drip bag? (In fact most of us worry that the FDA isn't protecting us enough because it is influenced by the corporations it's supposed to be regulating.) So why shouldn't we be protected from potentially toxic financial products?

What kind of protections did the five Wisconsin school districts deserve after losing more than $150 million while buying synthetic collateralized debt obligations? If there was no fraud involved, Milton Friedman would say, "Buyer beware." The officials were adults, and they should have known what they were doing. And truth be told, they are not entirely without fault. They no doubt were attracted to the higher rates of return embedded in their scheme, and therefore they should have known that higher rates meant higher risks. But when the top financial gurus of the country like Bernanke, Greenspan, and Soros all call these instruments "exotic and opaque," you wonder how a school official could possibly know enough. In Wisconsin, it was likely that neither the local broker, nor the most informed school officials, had any idea how synthetic collateralized debt obligations worked and what the risks actually were. It's highly doubtful that any financial advisor in the area would have known either. They needed protection *from* the "sound" advice they were getting. And when you realize that AIG bought billions of the same kind of synthetic CDOs as the Wisconsin schools purchased, it becomes clear that everyone needed protection.

Or did they? National Public Radio aired a disturbing interview with the reporters who helped produce the exposé on Whitefish Bay. When asked, "Is there an actual bad guy in this story?" NPR's Adam Davidson had a golden opportunity to slam CDOs and the other toxic derivatives that had infected public finance. Instead he said:

> There is a tragedy here too. Over the last thirty years, there have been a series of financial innovations that have just been plain good. They have allowed city governments, local governments, to get money more cheaply, which means more hospitals, more schools, better sewers, you know, just basic good public services, and that whole system may be permanently broken by this crisis. And that means, really for the foreseeable future, there's just going to be less public service in the U.S.[7]

I am stunned by this comment. What are these "just plain good" financial innovations? Certainly not the synthetic CDOs that have proven so lethal to the Wisconsin school districts. And the other innovations mentioned in his story, like "variable rate municipal bonds" backed by Depfa (the failed Irish bank that loaned money to Wisconsin and many other municipalities) also have soured.[8] But how can these wholesome "innovations" produce needed revenue and reduce costs only *some* of the time, and then at other times, these same financial innovations are able to cripple municipal finances for years to come? By any definition, that's speculation, not prudent municipal financing.

These "just plain good" financing tools were inherently risky from the git-go. They were sold *as if* their risk were minimal. It wasn't. These public agencies were able to raise money (for a time) at lower costs precisely because these risks remained hidden. When times were good, these public agencies won a few hands at the casino and could build "more hospitals, more schools, better sewers." Then, when the real risks emerged, the school districts and municipalities lost bets they didn't even know they had made. These municipalities, and others, are now building fewer hospitals and fewer schools, and letting their sewers decay, all as a result of those same "just plain good" financial innovations.

If these products went on trial, they would be found "guilty by design." They had no business being anywhere near public finance. The Orange County debacle should have taught us that nearly a decade ago. But the salespeople, the investment houses, and the banks collected enormous fees and pushed the risky products. The derivative gang feasted on the sweet public agency funds, like bears on a honey pot.

We should be worried indeed, if at this late date, one of the most able NPR reporters who has been investigating this story for months is still defending the wonders of CDOs and the like. All the more reason why we need to stop these dangerous products before they do more damage around the globe.[9]

Financial Product Safety Commission

Perhaps you agree that if these faulty financial products were prescription drugs, we'd demand careful testing before they were unleashed on the public. So why not develop an international body to approve and certify financial innovations before they are sold to unsuspecting buyers all over the planet?

Would forcing these derivatives to go through an FDA-like product-approval process have helped? That's a hard call. It is possible that in small quantities, a specific derivative creates value and can be safely bought and sold. The problem of systemic risk only emerges when there are hundreds of billions of dollars' worth circling the globe. But, under any circumstances are they appropriate investments for public agencies? It may be the case that we should limit the markets for these new investments so that public funds, pension funds, and endowments are off-limits. And in some cases the entire class of derivatives may have to be limited in order to prevent systemic risk. None of this will be easy to do.

But this is the time to try. The financial markets are in shambles. The economy is spiraling down. Banks, insurance companies, and even hedge funds are in severe distress. People are losing their jobs. Incomes are falling. State and local revenues are collapsing. We should review financial products before they do more damage.

We have allies in high places. Billionaire investor George Soros told the House Oversight and Government Reform committee on November 13, 2008, that the Obama administration should put a high priority on ensuring that new financial engineering products are approved by regulators. He argued that "financial engineering must also be regulated and new products must be registered and approved by the appropriate authorities before they can be used."[10]

However, such proposals face serious obstacles. For starters, they would require international cooperation. And then there's the question of how to find and retain regulators who are skilled enough to understand—let alone evaluate—these innovations. Soros has an interesting suggestion: If the derivative product is too opaque and difficult for regulators to comprehend, it should be banned from use. Not a bad notion. But we also need to do something about the revolving door to Wall Street's high salaries that shapes the career path of regulators. Besides, if we want a healthier economy and society, our system of compensation needs to be a lot less lopsided.

Next stop: Why tightening the growing wage gap between elites and the average working person is vital to our recovery.

| eleven |

Proposals Wall Street *Really* Won't Like

WHO ARE THE BIG WINNERS at the fantasy-finance casino? Many of the very richest people in America. In 1982, the top 400 individuals held an average net worth of $604 million each (in 2008 dollars). By 1995, their average wealth jumped to $1.7 billion. And in 2008, the 400 top winners averaged $3.9 billion *each.*[1] Just imagine. Your Lear Jet lands on the private runway out back and you are whisked to a gold-plated game room. You and 399 other multibillionaires take your drinks and settle into the plush leather chairs at the gaming tables. In front of each of you are your chips—3,900 of them, with each chip worth $1 million! The total for the 400 high rollers adds up to a cool $1.56 trillion. That's equal to about 10 percent of the entire gross domestic product of the United States.

Has fantasy finance been good to you or what?[2]

This year you sense the crackling excitement as the top 25 hedge fund managers arrive at the casino. In 2008, a year that saw the collapse of the stock market, the implosion of pension funds, 401(k)s, and college endowments, the destruction of millions of jobs, and the worst recession since the 1930s, the top 25 hedge fund managers received $11.6 billion in compensation. You join in the thunderous applause as these guests of honor waltz in.[3]

But just outside the window, if you dare to look, are 94.6 million nonsupervisory workers who earn less than the average worker did in 1973. Also out there are about 44 million Americans with no health care. They could use some of those chips. If each billionaire inside the casino walked out with "only" $100 million per person, they would leave $1.52 trillion sitting on the table. If these chips landed in the public coffers, let's say via steeply progressive income and wealth taxes, we could invest $150 billion a year in developing and deploying renewable energy alternatives—ten times what President Obama called for during his campaign. Or we could provide free tuition for every student at every public college and university—in perpetuity.

Yet, we Americans are skittish about redistribution. As President Obama said, "This is America. We don't disparage wealth. We don't begrudge anyone for achieving success."[4] In fact, we believe both in the equality of opportunity *and* in the inequality of income. Nearly all of us would agree that those who have talent, study hard, and work hard should earn more than those who don't. We admire the most successful in every field. We more or less agree that it's fine to be rich. Most of us would like to be rich as well. But we also have a sense of fairness. We worry when the gap between the superrich and the rest of us grows and grows, especially while most of us run in place. And there's that nagging feeling that the billionaire CEO who makes 1,000 times more money than his average employee isn't actually 1,000 times smarter, 1,000 times more studious, or 1,000 times harder working. In other words, the extent of inequality we see today in America cannot possibly be due to merit. It comes, largely, from those who are in the right positions at the right times to game the casino.

The more their wealth accumulates, the more the superrich are able to lobby for reducing taxes on capital gains, on inheritance, and on the highest incomes. In 2008, corporate recipients of our tax dollars, in the form of Troubled Asset Relief Program (TARP) bailouts, spent $77 million on lobbying and $37 million in campaign contributions. According to the Center for Responsive Politics, their return on that investment was 258,449 percent.[5] It's hard to get elected to anything without the financial backing of these elites. In fact, the best way to get elected is to be one of them.

We also worry that the superrich are severing their social

connections with the rest of us. They no longer live anywhere near us (or if they do, it is behind well-protected walls, fences, and gates). Their kids don't go to our schools. They don't ride on our buses and trains, and they're not in line with us at the airport either. They don't see our doctors or go to our hospitals. So they don't suffer the indignities of our crowded services and collapsing infrastructure. Do they have any idea what our lives are like?

After the December 2008 auto-industry bailout, Bob Lutz, the vice-chairman of GM, was suffering from culture shock. He found himself in a strange land—America. He had been forced to go native. "I've never quite been in this situation before of getting a massive pay cut, no bonus, no longer allowed to stay in decent hotels, no corporate airplane. I have to stand in line at the Northwest counter. I've never quite experienced this before. I'll let you know a year from now what it's like."[6]

Our sense that the rich have been pulling away from the rest of us is confirmed by the statistics. As chart 9 illustrates, in 1970 the gap between the top 100 CEOs' average pay and the pay of average workers was 45 to 1 ($296,170 to $6,542), reflecting the restraints of lingering New Deal financial controls and mores. As those controls weakened, the gap increased to 127 to 1 by 1980.

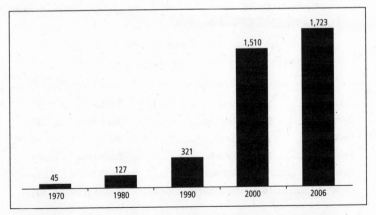

Chart 9. Ratio of Top 100 U.S. CEO Salaries to Average Worker Annual Earnings. CEO pay from "CEO Compensation Survey," *Forbes*, April or May issues, 1971–2008; earnings for workers from Bureau of Labor Statistics.

As deregulation, tax cuts, and the union bashing of the Reagan era took hold, the gap jumped to 321 to 1 by 1990. In 2000, as "financial innovation" pumped up fantasy finance, the ratio of CEO pay to the average workers' pay hit an obscene level of 1,510 to 1. And then by 2006, at the height of the fantasy-finance boom, it climbed to a whopping 1,723 to 1 ($50,877,450 to $29,529).

When it comes to the pay gap, we lead the world. Table 1 shows how the United States stacked up in 2000 measuring a broader group than in chart 9.

Of course not all these overpaid CEOs come from the financial sector. But the financial sector sets the pattern. And its sky-high salaries have lured some of our brightest minds away from other less lucrative fields in science and medicine or, God forbid, the humanities. As historian Niall Ferguson writes:

> Back in 1970 only around 5 percent of the men graduating Harvard, where I teach, went into finance. By 1990 that figure had risen to 15 percent. Last year the proportion was even higher. According to the Harvard Crimson, more than 20 percent of the men in the Class of 2007, and 10 percent of the women, expected their first jobs to be at banks. And who can blame them? In recent years, the pay packages in finance have been nearly three times the salaries earned by Ivy League graduates in other sectors of the economy.[7]

Japan	10	Spain	18	Britain	25
Germany	11	Belgium	19	Hong Kong	38
Switzerland	11	Italy	19	Mexico	45
Sweden	14	Canada	21	Argentina	48
New Zealand	16	Australia	22	South Africa	51
France	16	Netherlands	22	United States	495

Table 1. Ratio of CEO Compensation to Average Employee Compensation in 2000. Non-U.S. values from Michael Hennigan, "Executive Pay and Inequality in the Winner-take-all Society," Finfacts Ireland, August 7, 2005. U.S. value from author calculation based on Hennigan and BLS at www.bls.gov/oes/2000/oes_51PR.htm.

Why study the big bang when you can become a master of the universe with the money you make building fantasy-financial models? If you have the urge to teach Shakespeare, why not wait until you retire—early and rich?

How the hell did we let so much wealth go to so few people?

———

If this outrageous wage gap concerns you, now may be the best time in history to do something about it—starting with the financial sector. But first we need to understand why financial workers earn so much more than the rest of us. Are these bankers and derivative traders really worth more in a year than we can earn in a lifetime? Is there something special about the combination of brains, experience, skill, and entrepreneurial ability that truly accounts for the outsized compensation packages?

If you listen closely to bankers, financiers, and TV financial commentators, the word "smart" comes up a lot. It's all about working with the smartest people. If you can recognize the smart ones it implies that you must be smart too. But the only true measure of financial smarts is how much you make. If you're really smart, you'll earn more. And if you earn more, you must be really smart. (And if you don't buy this logic, by definition, you're not smart enough to earn more.)

Smart fits into human capital theory, which tells us that the more we invest in ourselves—and build up our human capital—the more money we should be able to fetch in the market. For instance, the further you go in school, the more you are likely to earn over your lifetime. Studies confirm a sizable and consistent gap between those who complete only high school and those who finish four years of college or more. But this doesn't explain why a banker should earn ten times more than a brain surgeon.

Robert Frank and Philip Cook, in The Winner-Take-All Society, believe that in our global marketplace, it's profitable to pay the very top performers much, much more than the next best. They point out that in a winner-take-all market, "High salaries are associated with positions that entail a great deal of leverage on the worker's efforts. In these positions small differences in performance translate into large differences in the profitability of the venture."[8] And if you apply this idea to the financial sector, as the value and volume of trade mushroomed, "The skills of any given salesman in this environment were suddenly given much greater leverage, so that one with exceptional flair and persuasiveness with customers was worth millions of dollars per year to the investment house."[9]

One of my high-finance soccer dads said he thought it had more to do with the sheer size of the industry. As he put it: "The world's money runs through New York and a few other money centers. The size of deals, trades, and sales is enormous. Even a very slight fee—let's say 3 basis points [three one-hundredths of 1 percent] of $100 billion in transactions—comes out to $30 million for the firm and for the bankers."

In their recent paper for the National Bureau of Economic Research, Thomas Philippos and Ariell Reshef applied statistical tests to various theories for why financial sector employees are paid so much more than other people. They find that neither modern technology, nor education, nor the higher risk of losing one's job on Wall Street can explain the disparity. Instead, they conclude that "financiers are overpaid."[10]

Even candid bankers will tell you that. But *why* are they overpaid?

Paul Krugman believes it has a great deal to do with social and political forces, especially unionization. He argues that "we had a society 25 years ago in which there were some constraints imposed by public opinion, by strong unions, by a general sense that there were things that you don't do. And maybe that led firms to make a decision to think of there being a sort of tradeoff between a 'let's have a happy high morale' workforce, or let's have a super star CEO and squeeze the workers for all we can."[11]

Krugman's right, but there's one more critical element: fantasy finance. When you are creating it, trading it, and unloading it, your earnings become fantastic—literally. When you get a cut of the biggest casino games ever created, your take will be huge. As economist Robert Reich put it: "[T]here's no reason to believe Wall Street executives have been smarter than executives in the real, non-financial economy. They've been paid more because they've been smarter at creating schemes that have only appeared to create value, while keeping investors in the dark.[12]

The President's Wage Cap

Can we really do anything about this? It won't be easy. We may already have reached a tipping point where the wealthy can so successfully control public policy that they will repel any serious effort to reduce the wage gap. But the public is growing angrier by the day, so this is the time to try. How about: *No salaries at these institutions shall be greater than that of the president of the United States?*

I wrote those words in October 2008. Then events passed me by. Within three months Wall Street awarded $18.4 billion in bonuses to itself. While these bonuses were actually for work done in 2007, they were paid out in 2008 and first reported in January 2009—after a year of record losses, and only months after receiving hundred of billions in federal bailout funds. Bad timing.

President Obama immediately called the bonus money "shameful," and the "height of irresponsibility." The next day Senator Claire McCaskill (D-Missouri), an Obama ally, proposed a $400,000 cap—the president's salary—for all executives whose firms receive government bailout funds. On February 5, 2009, the Obama administration called for a wage cap of $500,000 on top executives, not for all bailed-out firms, but only for those who receive "extraordinary help from U.S. taxpayers."[13] But there were plenty of loopholes that allowed large amounts of deferred compensation, and that limited the cap only to the top few executives. (To gain perspective on the enormity of this cap, many Wall Street executives and traders make more than that in *one week*—$500,000 per week, after all, equals "only" $26 million a year.)

Then events passed him by. On February 13, Congress added a stronger wage-cap provision to the $787-billion stimulus package—over the objections of the Obama administration. Responding to rising popular revulsion, the bill limited bonus money and deferred compensation to no more than one-third of salaries, and it covered all institutions that had or would receive bailout funds. The provisions not only would include the top five executives, but also the top twenty highest paid employees. The cap, therefore, would cover the stock, bond, and derivative traders who had earned tens of millions on their deals. Many of these elite traders are the ones who dreamed up and profited from the opaque and exotic games—the croupiers of the fantasy-finance casino.

The Obama administration seemed concerned that these provisions would cause a brain drain from the sector. Compensation consultants agreed. As one put it, "Those rules won't work. Any smart executive will (*a*) pay back TARP money ASAP or (*b*) get another job."[14]

But isn't that the whole idea? Paying back the taxpayer quickly is not a vice. And it might be virtuous if some of these smart folks applied their talents to other pressing issues like alternative energy, education, or health care.

Experts also worry that the talent will shift to hedge funds and foreign banks, taking their lucrative clients with them, and starting a downward spiral within banks that have accepted government funds. As one Wall Street consultant put it, "At some point you begin to wonder: has the government given up on these companies anyway? Why would the government or the White House want to go along with that unless they have come to the conclusion they will have to nationalize these firms anyway?"[15]

Obviously the Obama administration is not willing to take on the entire banking community, and is likely to seek modifications. It seems the president's primary intent is to use a combination of regulations plus the bully pulpit to drill a stronger sense of responsibility and sensitivity into the financial sector, without causing a massive brain drain. Good luck.

On this issue, Obama and his treasury secretary, Timothy Geithner, may be lagging behind Main Street. It seems, the average citizen is questioning the Wall Street definition of "smart," "valuable," and "talented." For those suffering or fearing economic hardships, the logic is straightforward: The bankers played at the high-stakes fantasy-finance casino and lost. Then they asked taxpayers for billions of dollars to cover their bets or else the economy would collapse even more than it was already doing. We gave them the money. But in return they can't scrape by on what the president of the United States is making?

Is this cap still too generous? Why should we allow struggling financial corporations to provide presidential-level benefits for their executives? After all, some pundits have even gone after *workers* in firms seeking a government rescue. *New York Times* business columnist Andrew Ross Sorkin blasted assembly-line autoworkers whose "gold-plated benefits are one reason why GM is no longer competitive." After citing misleadingly high estimates of the average auto worker's wages and benefits, he says workers shouldn't expect good health benefits when their employer is "asking the taxpayers—many of whom don't have health coverage—to pay your salary and health insurance."[16]

But Sorkin utters not a peep about the diamond-studded benefits of financial executives who already have been bailed out by taxpayers—benefits that far exceed anything an autoworker could hope for. Shouldn't we ask these bailed-out executives to give up their health coverage as well?

No. This race to the bottom has got to stop. The problem is not that autoworkers and the financial executives have "gold-plated" health care benefits. The problem is that so many Americans don't. This crisis should move us toward high-quality universal health care, like the rest of the industrialized world, not toward draconian cuts. If we had universal health care, a major burden would be removed from Detroit automakers and no one would be talking about depriving autoworkers or Wall Street executives of health care.

Maybe the president's salary cap will catch on. As the crisis deepens, Americans are discovering the ins and outs of elite compensation. It was a rude awakening to learn that AIG executives received $160 million in "retention bonuses" after their ruined company had hauled in about $170 billion in government bailouts. That's really hard to explain to an unemployed autoworker or a retired teacher in Miami trying to make her mortgage payments. It's possible that this anger could build into a more general call to cap top salaries in all firms that get big subsidies from the federal government—like military contractors.

If so, then Sam Pizzigati, a tireless labor activist, will get his due. For the past fifteen years he's been on a crusade for a *maximum* wage that caps executive pay at all companies to fifty times the lowest paid worker in the firm. (Remember, that's still a larger pay gap than in most countries, and than what it was during the "Golden Age" of American capitalism from the late 1940s to the early 1970s.) If the CEO wants a big raise, Sam argues, the CEO had better raise everyone's wages as well. Many of us thought this idea, while perhaps justified in theory, was too utopian for a modern economy. But Sam is starting to look like a hardheaded realist, just a little ahead of his time.[17]

I'm still a step behind. I'm not ready to push for an across-the-board cap. The public, I believe, would thoroughly reject it. However, we have a once-in-a-lifetime opportunity to reduce the wage gap on Wall Street. That's where the pay is most outrageous and harmful to the entire economy. Let's keep our focus on that enormous problem. As economist Robert Frank puts it:

> A money manager's pay depends primarily on the amount of money managed, which in turn depends on the fund's rate of return relative to other funds. This

provides strong incentives to invest in highly leveraged risky assets, which yield higher average returns. But as recent events have shown, these complex assets also expose the rest of us to considerable systemic risk.

On balance, then, the high pay that lures talent to the financial industry may actually cause harm. So if Congress wants to cap executive pay in financial institutions receiving bailout money, well and good.[18]

Slapping around the superrich as they hold their cups out is satisfying, but too easy. In fact, indulging our righteous indignation is a luxury we can't afford, especially if it diverts us from real solutions. The eminent French sociologist Emil Durkheim called it "ressentiment"—an expression of powerlessness that he believed the masses show toward the powerful. In the vernacular, it means we'd rather bitch about the rich than exercise more power and take more responsibility for ruling society. Bitching won't get regular workers a bigger piece of the pie or reduce fantasy finance's "super-senior slice." To do that, we need to cut off the supply of surplus capital that feeds fantasy finance.

As we discussed in chapter 2, productivity increases and wage increases were decoupled during the 1970s. As a result, trillions of dollars in surplus capital went to the investor class because average real wages failed to rise along with productivity. There was so much surplus capital held in so few hands that it could no longer find solid investments in the production of goods and services. (Had it gone to working people, there would have been more spending on real goods and services, and more investment opportunities in the real economy.) Instead, it then funneled into the fantasy-finance casino. Clouds of financial instruments were created to suck up the surplus capital, and this put us all at risk.

In 2004, economists Jamal Rashed and Subarna Samanta statistically tested whether this gap caused financial instability. They concluded that when the discrepancy between rising productivity and wage stagnation is large, "stock markets crash, banks fail, currencies depreciate, unemployment rises, and a longer recession or a full-fledged depression may follow." They predicted that "an increase in the productivity-wage gap over time should lead to 'irrational exuberance' in the stock market."[19] In fact, this was also the primary source of the housing bubble.

But why did productivity and wage increases diverge? Many economists say that workers' education levels didn't increase fast enough to keep pace with the jobs needed in a modern, technologically sophisticated economy. We need more technical professionals and fewer manual laborers and machine operators. But there are other factors that have more force. First, globalization opened up vast new labor markets overseas. Manufacturing, once the engine of America's middle-class incomes, shifted to countries with far lower labor costs. Even companies that didn't move overseas forced workers' wages down to compete with low-cost producers. People in the service sector also faced competition as call-center jobs and other white-collar work moved elsewhere. Trade agreements failed to take into account the different countries' vastly disparate labor and environmental laws and conditions. It became increasingly difficult for American workers to compete against labor markets in countries where union organizers were murdered, where health and safety conditions were deadly, and where companies could pollute the environment with abandon. The net result of all this was downward pressure on real wages of the average American worker, even while labor productivity increased.

Another reason wages have fallen behind is the dive in union membership and the accompanying decline of workers' collective-bargaining power. For many reasons, including legal obstacles that make it very difficult for workers who want a union to get one, a shrinking percentage of the workforce is represented by unions. (Chart 10 tracks unionization rates in the private sector. The rate including public-sector workers in 2008 is 12.4

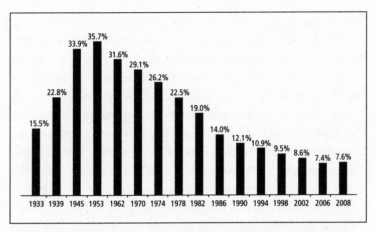

Chart 10. Percent of Private Sector Workers in U.S. Unions. Data from 1933–1982 come from Leo Troy and Neil Sheflin, *U.S. Union Sourcebook* (West Orange, NJ: IRDIS, 1985). Data for 1986–2008 are from Bureau of Labor Statistics, Employment and Earnings, January issues, 1987–2009.

percent, up from 12.1 percent in 2007.) Some argue that workers have rejected unions because of leadership's failure to be attentive to the members' needs. However, in most cases unions have lost members because the industries that they had unionized declined drastically or moved out of the country. This lower "union density" makes it harder for even organized workers to bargain for higher wages: They face competition not only globally but from low-wage, nonunion workers in this country. As labor declined, it lost much of its ability to affect the pace of globalization and the content of free-trade agreements.

It's time to stitch these patterns together to form one reasonably coherent explanation for the current crisis.

But first a word of extreme caution. The global economic system is enormously complex. Therefore, systemic explanations always should be offered with great humility. Most will be wrong. I recall a story from my late colleague Tony Mazzocchi (1926–2002), the visionary labor leader. At a labor-management pension-fund meeting Mazzocchi attended in the late 1990s, one of the consultants made a euphoric speech about the economy's "new paradigm." The consultant believed that we had reached a new era of perpetually rising stock markets. Hence, he argued the pension fund should bank on a higher rate of return for the indefinite future. Mazzocchi flashed a wily smile and asked, "Since when did they repeal the laws of capitalism?" Mazzocchi was right, of course. He had lived through the Depression and feared it could happen again. But I recall at the time thinking that maybe Mazzocchi was wrong. Maybe something about the structure of capitalism really had changed so that extreme booms and busts were a thing of the past. Go figure.

Have I finally figured out all the laws of capitalism?[20] No. But I am sure of one: We can count on more booms and busts. So, I offer this explanation:

- Because productivity and real worker wages diverged starting in the 1970s, income gushed to the top—to the richest 1 percent or so among us. Tax cuts for the wealthy, deregulation, globalization, antiunion policies, reduced social programs, and declining value of the minimum wage all accelerated that process. The productivity bonus went to the investor class instead of to workers, where it had gone between 1945 and 1973.
- Some of that capital went to productive investments. But eventually it ran out of moderate-risk investment opportunities in the real economy. It became surplus capital when it could no longer find stable investments to make in the real economy.
- The problem of surplus capital that couldn't find a home was "solved" by the derivative industry. CDO-type investments offered higher rates of return, supposedly at little risk. The casino was open for business.
- Through the magic of fantasy-finance derivatives, these funds were recycled to cover risky consumer and corporate debt, and to create instruments that

were leveraged again and again upon these debts. All this was enormously profitable for the financial firms that arranged, sold, and traded these products. It also made hundreds of billions of dollars available both for housing and credit card debt and for additional fantasy-finance betting. The surplus capital fueled the housing boom via the derivatives, and it led to a vast expansion of the financial sector.

- Meanwhile, working families had to work harder and longer to make ends meet. More and more families needed two wage earners. More families increased their debt loads.

- The bubble burst because that's what bubbles do. At some point marginal buyers could no longer buy enough houses or pay for the ones they had bought. Too many builders built too many homes because the boom had accelerated prices. American workers with stagnating real wages had reached their debt limits and could no longer fuel the boom.

- When the housing bubble burst, the entire fantasy-finance edifice that had been built upon it collapsed as well. Investors and banks all over the globe were loaded with toxic derivatives based on risky mortgages that had crashed in value. The risk supposedly had been engineered out of these derivatives, but it hadn't. Many financial institutions central to the economy became insolvent or nearly so. The banking system froze. The stock market crashed. The global economy tanked.

And here we are.

———

Whether or not this summary gets the story exactly right, there are strong reasons to narrow the wage gap as a way of dealing with the ongoing crisis. If real wages rise, workers will spend more money in the real economy and the superrich will have less money to spend on speculative investments. With more money in their pockets, workers will increase the demand for goods and services, and fewer of them will default on their mortgages.

Another good reason to raise workers' wages is to guard against deflation. In October 2008 consumer prices dropped one full percent—the biggest decline since the Great Depression. Then in November it dropped another 1.7 percent, setting another record. (Fortunately, the drops mitigated over the next few months as prices began slowly to rise again.) But if price declines do take hold, we're in serious trouble. Deflation is a sustained, overall drop in prices. It happens when demand for goods and services declines because of a systemic crisis like the one we're going through. If you're losing your job or fear you might soon, you hold back on purchases. If you see millions of people losing their jobs you're not going to go on a spending spree. And when you notice that prices are falling, you might delay buying something, especially a big-ticket item, because you're hoping prices will fall even further. All of this further reduces demand, which causes economic activity to slow. Investment and consumption continue to fall, more workers lose their jobs, prices drop some more, and we get stuck in a deflationary spiral. This describes the Great Depression. We don't want to go there again. One of the very best antidotes is to move more money into the hands of working people—the sooner the better.

Employee Free Choice Act

The New Deal came about in part because of pressure from a growing labor movement. And the New Deal itself further strengthened unions. New Deal policy makers believed that, as union members, working people would have a better chance at getting their fair share of productivity. Roosevelt welcomed a new wave of union organizing. He supported the Wagner Act, which made it much easier for workers to unionize. And history shows that the plan worked: Postwar unionization did boost workers' real wages—and in a way that was perfectly compatible with innovation and profits for business owners. We could do it again by passing the Employee Free Choice Act, now before Congress.[21]

Since the late 1940s, labor law has been whittled away—and employers have become increasingly aggressive in squelching union drives. Workers who try to organize a union are routinely harassed or even fired. For unions, it has become extremely costly and difficult to conduct an organizing drive. Without question the playing field has been tilted toward employers. Cornell University professor Kate Bronfenbrenner found in a survey of NLRB election campaigns in 1998 and 1999 that employers illegally fired employees for union activity in 25 percent of organizing drives.[22] An updated study done by the Center for Economic and Policy Research estimates that in 2007, one in five union organizers or activists was illegally fired during organizing drives.[23]

It's estimated that about 60 million Americans would like to join a union. If we remove the roadblocks, many of them could. And then they could win better wages and safer working conditions—at least 50,000 American workers die from job-related injuries or disease every year.[24] Even if EFCA doesn't result in a sudden rise in unionization, nonunion firms are likely to raise wages just to keep workers from turning to unions.[25] And rising wages will stabilize our economy. Working people will stop holding back on spending, and that will chase deflation away. The Chamber of Commerce ought to promote unionism—it was good for business in years past and would be good for business again today.

Raising the Minimum Wage

A higher minimum wage would also guard against deflation and direct additional wealth away from the casino. And it's the right thing to do. No one can live a decent life at the current minimum wage, which rises from $6.55 to $7.25 in 2009. If you adjust for inflation you can see that the real buying power of the minimum wage peaked in 1979 at about $8.89 in current dollars (see chart 11). This is an excellent time to jump the minimum wage to at least $10 an hour and index it permanently to infla-tion. (For those worried about potential job loss, see studies by David Carr and Alan Kreuger.)[26]

Will raising real wages through unionization and increasing the minimum wage actually pull us out of this crisis? We won't know until we try. But we do know what happened when we let real wages decline—the top 1 percent ended up with more money than they knew what to do with. We tried deregulation and got "exotic and opaque derivatives" and the worst financial meltdown since the Great Depression. We tried trickle down and it widened the income gap. We tried to encourage investment by and for the rich, and we got a fantasy-finance boom and a slew of billionaires. We created a finance-heavy economy that was supposed to be the wave of the future. Instead we got a taste of the past—a near 1930s depression. Let's find out what happens

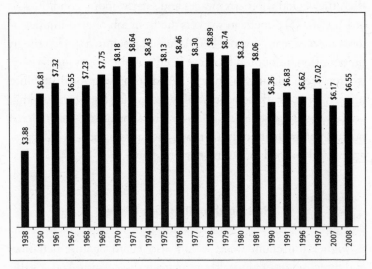

Chart 11. The Minimum Wage Adjusted for Inflation (2008 dollars). Adapted from U.S. Department of Labor, Wage and Hour Division.

if we allow middle class and lower-income people to earn decent wages.

It's not that these two changes can guarantee that we will never have another financial crash. They can't. No amount of reform can guarantee that, as long as we have a free-enterprise financial sector. But the occasional mild recession is not what we're worried—and angry—about. It's the wild swings of excess and catastrophe that need taming. And unionization and a livable minimum wage *will* go a long way in moving us toward that goal.

This is the time to try these pro-worker strategies precisely because the financial world is changing so dramatically. Our financial elites have wheedled the government into handing the banking industry over a trillion dollars. More corporate handouts are sure to come. The orthodoxy of deregulation—embraced for years by both Republicans and Democrats—is being trashed by many of the very policy makers who once touted it. Right now, it's going to be hard for financial leaders to argue that the minimum wage, unions, and fairer trade agreements interfere with free markets. We've needed a new direction for decades. Now is the best chance we'll ever have to make it happen. Let us learn from the bankers and take bold action while we can.

———

We've come full circle since our initial tour of Whitefish Bay, Wisconsin. To date, the town seems to be surviving its flirtation with fantasy finance. Its mansions still tower over Lake Michigan. Its middle-class neighborhoods don't look the worse for wear. The doors of its art deco movie theater on Silver Spring Drive are still open, as are the tasty-foods shops. And, its white-collar residents still care deeply about its schools. But its pride, as well as its coffers, have been wounded at the fantasy-finance casino.

Local school officials had hoped that fantasy finance would enrich their school systems, not themselves. But they played a game they didn't understand. They were enticed into buying a financial weapon of mass destruction—a synthetic collateralized debt obligation—the exotic and opaque financial instrument so key in crashing our economy. They were romanced by the purveyors of the fantasy-finance dream, and they fell for it head over heels. The courts will decide whether they were illegally deceived and deserve redress. But obviously they were taken in, as was our entire economy.

Our out-of-control privatized financial system created, marketed, and peddled junk dreams. It's very tempting to blame individuals for the years of outrageous profiteering, speculative borrowing, lending, and investing. In Wisconsin we could point to the town officials who should have known better, the brokers who led them down a risky path, the investment houses that cooked up the risky deals, and the bankers, here and abroad, who profited so handsomely from the junk securities. Columnist David Brooks suggests that the big unanswered question of the crash of 2008 is "how so many people could be so stupid, incompetent and self-destructive all at once."[27]

A good question—but not the most productive one for understanding this crisis. We will not find the root causes of the global financial meltdown in our irrational psyches, in our bad behavior, or even in our greedy financiers. Instead, we should examine our privatized financial system. Why is it so unstable? And how can it be stabilized?

We've heard the wisdom of philosophers and prophets who, for over five thousand years, have worried that money-making-money disrupts the social order. They feared that indebtedness would lead to poverty and inequality (which it does), and that unfettered finance would cause social instability (which it does). We saw that as capitalism matured into a global system, political economists tried to understand and tame destructive booms and busts, and to draw a line between sound investing and casino gambling, between risk-taking and recklessness. These economists hoped to foster the intrepid entrepreneurial spirit that created new wealth, while discouraging the gambling that caused instability. Unfortunately, their attempts largely failed. Perhaps that's because in the private financial sector, risk-taking and recklessness are intractably entwined.

Economists John Maynard Keynes and Hyman Minsky believed that our privatized financial system was inherently unstable—that it would always wobble between booms and busts.[28] As Minsky wrote, the "instability of financial markets—the periodic crunches, squeezes, and debacles—. . . is a normal functioning internally generated result of the behavior of a capitalist economy."[29] Although critical of the status quo, these economists believed deeply in the overall value of the capitalist system. But they saw an enormous difference between markets for goods and services and financial markets. They thought that decentralized free markets were much more efficient and productive that any state-run system could ever be. Like Milton Friedman, they believed that the free market protected and enhanced individual freedoms and offered people opportunity. Like New Deal Democrats, they also believed capitalism could promote social justice and increase equality. But while they extolled the virtues of decentralized markets for producing and distributing goods and services, they had seen that private financial markets could melt down and lead to severe depressions.

In this book, we sought to pinpoint and demystify the financial instruments that promoted our latest bout of financial instability. Of course, these products were not solely responsible for the crash. But they contributed mightily to systemic risk by lining up a fragile set of global financial dominoes. Early on, people on Wall Street began calling these financial instruments "toxic waste." But they had no idea how toxic and wasteful they would become.

In these last chapters we've suggested ways to protect ourselves from financial instability: financial-disaster insurance, the president's wage cap, financial-engineering controls, unionization, and increasing real wages and the minimum wage. These reforms would shift resources to the real economy and away from fantasy finance. But even these proposals may not be sufficient.

It may be time to look more closely at the most radical proposals offered by Keynes and Minsky. To protect our decentralized
capitalist system from collapse, they thought it might be necessary to "socialize" the largest pieces of the private financial
sector. Not temporarily "pre-privatize" them, but socialize them
for good. A few years ago this would have seemed absolutely
outrageous. The major banks, insurance companies, and investment houses were wildly profitable and seemed to be dynamic
engines of economic growth. They were attracting our most able
minds. They were minting new wealth for their employees and
stockholders.

But now these same institutions are in shambles—even after
we've bailed them out with our billions. It was not a cabal of
socialists who began nationalizing these institutions. It was the
ultraconservative, free-market Bush administration. It realized
that without massive intervention, these banks would fail, taking
the entire financial system with them. If the government hadn't
begun its stutter-step program of nationalization, we might
already be deep into Great Depression II.

The public now, more or less, owns Freddie and Fannie, AIG,
Citigroup, and a good deal of Bank of America as well. Soon
other banks will be begging us for bailouts. We are becoming the
saviors of all the financial institutions that are too big to fail, but
are failing anyway. Yet we seem afraid to take over these institutions, or even hold them strictly accountable for how they spend
our money.

We now face a set of fateful choices. We can hold onto and
supervise the semi-socialized financial sector, or we can return
the entire banking system to private investors. We can enact
policies that allow workers' real wages to rise, or we can keep the
wealth flowing upward to the superrich. We can put limits on
financial engineering, or we can wait and see what the next orgy
of fantasy finance does to our economy.

Policy makers face deep political crosscurrents. Many will try
to avoid these stark choices by steering a middle path. They don't

want to nationalize more banks. And they want to return the ones we own to the private sector as soon as possible.

When the government first began its bailout effort, its aim was simply to rid the banks of their toxic assets, like a giant financial superfund cleanup project. But then they decided this fix wouldn't be fast enough. So instead they tried to get banks lending again (and aid bank stockholders) by pumping in hundreds of billions in cash, along with billions more in asset guarantees. But this cash came with virtually no strings attached. And soon the feds discovered that the banks were using our money to sit tight, pay bonuses and dividends, and buy up other companies. As one banker defiantly put it in January 2009, after receiving $300 million from the federal bailout: "Make more loans? We're not going to change our business model or our credit policies to accommodate the needs of the public sector as they see it to have us make more loans."[33]

As of this writing, the Obama administration is unveiling a new plan that insures investors who are being encouraged to buy the toxic assets and get them off the books of the crippled banks. But no one knows what this financial toxic waste is genuinely worth, and so it's unclear just how much of a risk Obama is taking with taxpayer money, or how much of a windfall his plan will be for these insider investors. Also, the definition of "toxic" will get increasingly murky as financial assets lose value during the deep economic recession. The price tag for our largesse for the banks could reach the trillions.

And all because we are tiptoeing around nationalization. We fear it conjures up vast bureaucracies staffed with do-nothing civil servants who will screw it up. But could they really screw it up more than the private-sector bankers already have?

Some fear that a full-scale financial takeover will scare away investors and further depress the stock market—the global symbol of financial health. But why should we continue to protect investors who bet big on junk, profited immensely, and then turned to us for help?

Some fear being called socialists by conservative pundits, even though the Cold War is long gone. But if banks continue to spiral down and threaten the entire economy, isn't it time to say that the only thing about nationalization we have to fear is fear itself?

Perhaps the biggest problem with our government's avoidance of nationalization is that the alternatives may not work. We are gambling that somehow, the hodgepodge of bailouts, regulations, and stimulus bills will get us out of the current mess. The odds are even longer that these measures will eliminate long-term financial instability. History provides little reassurance. Never before has so much human energy been devoted to investigating, analyzing, and managing our economy. And yet the most advanced and sophisticated economic system ever created crashed all over our research papers, our econometric models, and our free-market theories, not to mention our real lives. And the odds are, if we don't change the way we do things, it will crash again.

Alan Greenspan not only agrees, but considers these crashes a small price to pay for all that we have achieved. On the CNBC documentary "House of Cards," first aired on February 12, 2009, he readily admitted that greed was the fundamental economic motivation that drove the economy—both up and down. Moreover, he argued, we would have to live with it, because greed would always be with us, and it could never be legislated away. Like Solomon he weighed the productivity of capitalism against its periodic destructiveness:

> This is one of the most extraordinary things about this whole episode. Looking at the way we all behaved— how is it possible that this species built up such an extraordinary world standard of living, which has drawn hundreds of millions of people out of poverty? The thing we should be most extraordinarily appreciative of is how far this system has carried us. Because there is no doubt that somewhere in the future we are going to have

this conversation again. It will not be for quite a period of time, but it will occur because the flaws are such in human nature that we cannot change that—it doesn't work.[34]

But the choice is not between changing human nature and accepting unregulated free markets. Also, the choice is not between total socialism and unfettered capitalism. Given the vast complexities of our global economic system, we need to make room for more nuanced alternatives. Free-enterprise principles can govern most of our markets for goods and services, while we also tightly control finance. We need to square up to reality. The financial sector, when measured by its overall impact on our economic world, produces systemic instability and runs inefficiently when structured as a small set of for-profit enterprises that are too big to fail. At the very least we need some sort of way to protect ourselves from the crises that even Alan Greenspan has "no doubt" will occur again, such as the proposal for financial disaster insurance in chapter 10. But our children and grandchildren deserve better than the very least we can do.

Let's hope we won't throw away much of our children's inheritance because we did not have the courage to do the obvious: Take over the failing major banks, drastically trim their astronomical salaries, control their hazardous financial engineering, and run the damn things for the good of us all.

Once again, events may be passing me by. Each day we hear more and more references to nationalization. Economists, both from the left and right, are advocating temporary government ownership of failed banks (euphemistically called "pre-privatization"). A consensus is building rapidly, not because of ideology, but out of desperation. Obama's toxic-asset public-private partnership plan released in March 2009 is the last effort to avoid that strategy. If it fails, he might be forced to reach for the only option left on the table. But even among the strident critics, few, if any, seem willing to let the government run key financial institutions for the long haul. It seems that we'd rather gamble yet again on unstable private markets.

If, by the time you read these words, we have avoided a full-scale depression, we should consider ourselves more fortunate than wise. Or as Bob Dylan lamented,

> An' here I sit so patiently
> Waiting to find out what price
> You have to pay to get out of
> Going through all these things twice.[35]

Glossary

*Note: italicized terms within a glossary entry
have their own entries in the glossary.*

arbitrage: According to Investopedia.com it is "The simultaneous purchase and sale of an asset in order to profit from a difference in the price. It is a trade that profits by exploiting price differences of identical or similar financial instruments, on different markets or in different forms. Arbitrage exists as a result of market inefficiencies; it provides a mechanism to ensure prices do not deviate substantially from fair value for long periods of time."[1] So-called regulatory arbitrage means moving an investment from a form that is heavily regulated to one that is less regulated in order to profit from the weaker regulations.

collateralized debt obligation: A collateralized debt obligation, or CDO, is an artificial security created by financial engineers. It bundles together a pool of similar loans into securities that can be bought or sold. An investor that buys into a CDO owns a right to a part of this pool's interest income and principal. For example, a bank might pool together 5,000 different mortgages, car loans, and credit card debts into a CDO. An investor who purchases a *tranche* of the CDO would be paid a portion of the interest owed by the 5,000 borrowers in the pool. The investors in the CDO run the risk that some borrowers won't pay back their loans. But the risk is supposedly dispersed by bundling together so many loans. The interest rate paid to investors varies by the odds that the borrowers whose loans make up the CDO will default on their payments.[2] The more of that risk an investor is willing to take on, the higher the interest income for their tranche.

- **CDO squared:** For more serious gamblers only. You take riskiest *equity tranches* from a bunch of different pools of debt. You put them into their own new pool. You chop up that pool into *tranches* and sell the pieces just like you would a CDO. The highest slices of a CDO squared would be first in line to get the interest payments, but last in line for defaults. The equity tranche of a CDO squared would be last in line for the income and first in line to suffer losses from defaults. But the entire CDO squared faces much more risk than a normal CDO.

- **CDO cubed:** For wild-eyed gamblers who won't leave the roulette table until a fire burns down the casino. You take riskiest *tranches* from a bunch of *CDO-squared* pools and put them into a new pool and tranche that one up. It's hard to believe anyone would make, sell, or buy such a thing. Let me know if you find one.

credit default swap (CDS): A *derivative* security that shifts risk from a party that doesn't want the risk to a party that is willing to accept it . . . for a price. Basically it is like an insurance policy. You can insure a bond that you own with someone else (called the "counterparty") by paying that person a certain amount of money, just like paying insurance premiums. If the bond goes into default, that other person has to make you whole so that you don't lose anything on the defaulted bond. They don't call this insurance because insurance is regulated but CDSs are not.

But it is also very different from insurance as we know it. You and your counterparty can enter into a credit-default-swap agreement even if neither of you own the bond or item you're insuring. It is very much like taking out an insurance policy on a house that you don't own. People draw up these agreements on corporate bonds they don't own. They even do this to make bets on the weather. You can do a CDS to bet on absolutely anything as long as you can find a counterparty. These securities are unregulated. There may be from $60 trillion to $600 trillion worth of them around the world.

credit rating agencies: There are three primary ratings agencies in the United States: Moody's, Standard and Poor's, and Fitch's. They basically assign ratings that measure the credit worthiness of stocks, bonds, and other forms of debt. They also rate the credit worthiness of many institutions, including financial institutions. The higher the rating, the less a corporation, government agency, or country will have to pay in interest to raise money through the issuing of debt. In the United States, these ratings are given special status by government agencies. Their ratings, in effect, determine what financial instruments are appropriate for investment by pension funds and other public funds.

debt pool: To have a better opportunity to spread out risk, debt instruments like mortgages, credit cards, auto loans, and the like are put into large groupings called pools. The owners of such pools hope to control their potential losses due to default by owning a large pool of such debt.

derivative: A type of financial instrument whose value is derived from something else, called the underlying or referenced stock, bond, or other financial instrument. For example, a stock index is a derivative based on a group of underlying stocks. When you buy an index, you are not buying the stocks that make up that index. Yet your index security goes up and down based on the value of the stocks it tracks. This is different from owning a share of a mutual fund. In such a fund you actually own a piece of a pool of real stocks and bonds.

Think of fantasy baseball. It's a derivative game of betting based on statistics based on the behavior of real major league players. You don't own the real players, or even a piece of them as in a mutual fund. When you own a fantasy baseball team, you don't really own anything except your derivative statistics compiled for you by a service. Yet your bet has value because other players and their derivative teams are willing to bet with you. There can be tens of thousands of fantasy baseball leagues based on only the two major leagues. Similarly, there are tens of thousands of derivative securities based on combinations of the same underlying real securities. Most of the financial instruments described in this book, the *collateralized debt obligation*, *synthetic CDO*, *credit default swap*, *CDO squared*, and so on, are derivatives.

equity: In real estate it means the difference between what your house and property is worth and how much you owe on it. (If it is worth more than you owe, then you have equity. If it is worth less than you owe, you have "negative equity.") It also refers to the ownership interest in a corporation, usually in terms of stock or preferred shares, and it can more generally refer to stock market investments. In a brokerage account, equity is what your shares are worth if you sold them right now (minus any money you borrowed to buy them).

financial securities: Financial instruments representing financial value that you can buy and sell. Securities are broadly categorized into debt securities, such as federal notes, bonds, and securities like common stocks that represent a share of ownership in a company.[3] Financial engineers spend their time dreaming up new securities, some of which have turned out to be disastrous for our economy.

hedge fund: Investopedia.com describes a hedge fund as more or less "a mutual fund for rich people."[4] They use sophisticated methods and lots of *leverage* to accumulate income. You've got to be a sophisticated investor and be worth over a million dollars to invest in such a fund. The *Washington Post* reports that "As many as 2,000 of 10,000 hedge funds closed last year [2008] as clients redeemed their investments, according to various industry estimates. And the total amount of assets invested in hedge funds worldwide was cut nearly in half to $1.9 trillion."[5] For the most part they are unregulated, but the Obama administration is changing that.

investment banks: This is a complex financial institution that helps government agencies, countries, and corporations raise capital. It helps them issue stocks and bonds. It also helps to arrange and facilitate corporate mergers and acquisitions of other corporations. They also invent, buy, and sell new financial instruments like *collateralized debt obligations* and *credit default swaps*.

leverage: The use of financial instruments to borrow money so that you can increase the size of your investments. The more leverage, the more risk you are taking on. For example, a mortgage allows you to leverage your down payment. If you put down 20 percent on a $100,000 house and borrow 80 percent, you are leveraged 4 to 1. If the value of your house goes up $20,000, your investment has increased by 100 percent. But if it declines by $20,000, your equity has been wiped out. Some *hedge funds* and banks were leveraged 30 to 100 times their equity. When those investments soured, they lost billions because of the high ratio of leveraging.

moral hazard: in the context of the financial crisis, a term used to signify the perils of bailing out institutions that are too big to fail. If large institutions know they will be bailed out, economists argue, they will take greater risks than they would if they were subject to the market discipline of prospective failure.

prime, subprime, and Alt-A loans: Roughly speaking there are three types of borrowers—those with good credit histories (prime), those with poor credit histories (subprime), and those who may have good credit but don't want to document their income on loan applications (Alt-A). Usually a FICO credit score of 640 is the dividing line. (FICO is the widely used credit rating produced by Fair Isaac and Company that supposedly measures how likely you are to pay your bills. The higher the number the more credit worthy you are.)

productivity: It is a measure of the output of our economy divided by the hours worked in our economy. Output is usually measured by the Gross Domestic Product, the standard measure of the value of all the goods and services we produce in the country.

quants: Short for "quantitative analysts." In this book the term refers to those who do the mathematical and statistical work to determine risk and profitability of financial instruments like *derivatives*.

short selling: Selling a stock you don't own today and promising to deliver it on a specific date in the future, say thirty days from now. You are gambling that the stock price will drop between now and thirty days from now so that you can buy it more cheaply. In theory, the share you buy goes to the person you made the short sale to. The difference between your short sale today and what you end up buying the share for within the next thirty days is your profit or loss. Obviously, short sales are highly profitable when you think the market is going down, and then it does.

synthetic collateralized debt obligation: This *financial security* is a combination of a *collateralized debt obligation* and a *credit default swap*. It creates an artificial CDO (*tranches* and all) without assembling or owning the underlying *debt pool*. Instead credit default swaps are used. A counterparty provides insurance payments to the synthetic CDO to protect various kind of debt. The investor buys tranches of the synthetic CDO. The investor's money goes into a fund that insures the counter-party's debt. If that debt defaults, the investors in the riskiest tranche of the synthetic CDO are the first to lose their money, and so on up the tranches. The great advantage of the synthetic CDO is that it can be created quickly without the muss, fuss, and expense of buying up a pool of debt.

systemic risk: Financial risk can be divided into several kinds. Bankers take risks when they make specific loans. Investors take risks when they invest in the bank. But systemic risk is when a series of individual loan and investment risks string together to harm the financial system and the economy as a whole. The collapse, or near collapse, of several major financial institutions in 2008 froze the credit system as a whole and produced a deep economic recession. Those practices and financial instruments that caused the meltdown posed systemic risk.

tranche: The French word for "slice." It usually refers to the different slices of a *collateralized debt obligation* that is based on a *debt pool*. (But these days pundits and politicians use it as much as they can to show they're financially knowledgeable.) Usually there are three main slices: equity, mezzanine, and senior.

- **senior tranche:** The group of securities (it could be one large security or many smaller ones) that is first in line to receive the interest payments from the entire pool of debt. Therefore securities that come from the senior tranche are mostly protected from default. But as a result of lower risk exposure, they receive a lower interest rate.
- **mezzanine tranche:** The group of securities that is next in line to be paid from the entire pool's interest collections on the debt. It is therefore more risky than a security from the senior tranche. As a result, it gets a higher rate of return.

- **equity tranche:** This is the gambler's slice—the bottom slice of the pool. Securities from this group are last in line to receive interest payments from the pool of debt, and first in line to take the losses from defaults. Securities from the equity tranche, therefore receive a very high rate of return, assuming the defaults don't wipe it out entirely. (It's called the equity slice because equity holders are the last to have a claim on assets in case of a corporate default.)

Notes

Introduction

1. Megan Davies and Walden Siew, "45 Percent of World's Wealth Destroyed: Blackstone CEO," Reuters, March 10, 2009, at www.reuters.com/article/newsOne/ idUSTRE52966Z20090310.
2. U.S. Consumer Product Safety Commission, "PC Notebook Computer Batteries Recalled Due to Fire and Burn Hazard," October 30, 2008, at www .cpsc.gov/cpscpub/prerel/prhtml09/ 09035.html.
3. David Leonhardt, "Punctured Bubblenomics," *New York Times*, September 20, 2008, at www.nytimes.com/2008/09/21/weekinreview/21leonhardt.html.
4. From the "Fortune 500" at http://money.cnn.com/magazines/fortune/ fortune500/ 2008/full_list/.

Chapter 1: The Hooking of Whitefish Bay

1. Shaun Yde, "An Op-Ed Piece from Shaun Yde," at www.schoollawsuitfacts. com/2008/12/op-ed-piece-from-shawn-yde.html.
2. "Stifel Nicolaus: About Us," at www.stifel.com/include.asp?pgid=178, accessed on April 6, 2009.
3. Charles Duhigg and Carter Dougherty, "The Reckoning: From Midwest to MTA, Pain from Global Gamble," *New York Times*, November 1, 2008, at www .nytimes.com/2008/11/02/business/02global.html.
4. See video of Waukesha School Board Meeting, August 30, 2006, at http://www .youtube.com/watch?v=OydC6K0Dwjg.
5. "School Districts Seek $200 Million from Brokerage Firms," at www.school lawsuitfacts.com/2008/09/contact-craig-peterson-zigman-joseph.html.
6. Videotape of Kenosha School District financial committee meeting, May 8, 2007 (at 21:10 min.).
7. In the end, the five school districts to invest through Noack were Whitefish Bay, Kenosha, Kimberly, Waukesha, and West Allis–West Milwaukee.
8. In the Kenosha district, for example, the workers covered included teachers, educational support personnel, secretaries, custodial staff, electricians, carpenters, painters, and all of the administrators.
9. According to Investopedia.com "It is important to note that with a moral obligation bond, the additional security provided by the government is only morally—and not legally—binding. However, the pledge is generally regarded as being as credible as a legally binding promise because the issuing government would face negative credit rating effects if it failed to honor the pledge." In the case of the River Square Parking Garage in Spokane, Washington, in 1998, the default on moral obligation bonds led to the downgrading of all of Spokane's debt and to drawn-out lawsuits. Spokane has authorized the issue of binding general revenue bonds to settle the suits. See www.publicbonds.org/public_fin/ default.htm.
10. Videotape of Kenosha school district financial committee meeting, May 8, 2007 (at 25:15).
11. To be fair, at the May 22, 2007, Kenosha board meeting, Mr. Hujik announced he was going to vote against a motion to take out a $20 million line of credit

for the trust. He wanted more time to understand it. Everyone agreed and the motion was tabled. It came up again on June 26, 2007, and passed unanimously.

12. Tape of Kenosha school district finance committee meeting, May 8, 2007 (at 23:00).
13. Duhigg and Dougherty.
14. Ibid.
15. The districts received only minimal information on these complex investments. For example, on page 5 of a paper Stifel Nicolaus gave to the districts, dated July 26, 2006, there's a chart labeled "Synthetic CDO Flowchart" that describes a few of the properties of synthetic CDOs in general. But it would take someone with a great deal of experience to understand synthetic CDOs from that chart. What does jump out is that the Trust would receive "AA Notes," and that they would be connected to the "Investment Grade Corporate Debt" of "100+ companies" that were diverse in location and industry. In short, the flow chart makes it seem as if the investment was in a large, diversified pool of AA investment-grade securities—much like a mutual bond fund of corporate debt. This was not the case.
16. "Warren Buffet on Derivatives, Edited Excepts from Berkshire Hathaway Annual Report, for 2002" at www.fintools.com/docs/Warren%20Buffet%20 on%20Derivatives.pdf.
17. "School Districts Seek $200 Million from Brokerage Firms."
18. Gary Kunich, "Ask Feds to Cover CDO: Union" Kenosha News, February 1, 2009, at www.kenoshanews.com/scripts/edoris/edoris. dll?tem=lsearchart&search_iddoc=4290978
19. Noack is cooperating with the school districts and is not being sued.
20. Duhigg and Dougherty.
21. Ibid.

Chapter 2: The Iron Law of Fantasy Finance

1. Emmanual Saez, "Striking it Richer: The Evolution of Top Incomes in the United States (Update using 2006 preliminary estimates)," March 15, 2008, from Figure 2, "Decomposing the Top Decile US Income Share into 3 Groups, 1913–2006," p. 7, at http://elsa.berkeley.edu/~saez/saez-UStopincomes-2006prel.pdf.
2. Ellen R. McGrattan and Richard Rogerson, "Changes in the Distribution of Family Hours Worked Since 1950," Federal Reserve Bank of Minneapolis, Research Department Staff Report 397, April 2008, p. 6, at www.minneapolis-fed.org/research/SR/SR397.pdf.
3. Greg Ip and Mark Whitehouse, "Huge Flood of Capital to Invest Spurs World-Wide Risk Taking: Corporate and Foreign Savings Chase Assets, Driving Prices Up, Keeping Returns Low 'A Global Game of Chicken'," Wall Street Journal, November 3, 2005, p. 1, at http://newsgroups.derkeiler.com/Archive/Misc/misc .invest.stocks/2005-11/msg00223.html.

Chapter 3: Is There a Dime's Bit of Difference between Wall Street's "Innovation" and Gambling?

1. Marc Van De Mieroop, "The Invention of Interest," in The Origin of Value: The Financial Innovations that Created Modern Capital Markets, William N. Goetzmann and K. Geert Rouwenhorst, eds. (New York: Oxford University Press, 2005), p. 19.

2. Hammurabi Code of Laws, #48, at www.sacred-texts.com/ane/ham/ham05.htm.

3. Aristotle's *Politics* (350 B.C.) translated by Benjamin Jowett, at www.econ161. berkeley.edu/teaching_Folder/Econ_210a_f99/Readings/Aristotle_Politics_ brief.html.

4. "Aristotle's View Against Usury" at www.moneymuseum.com/standard_english/ raeume/geld_machen/bank/interest/aristotle/aristotle.html.

5. Muhammed A. Asadi, "The Koran, Interest & the Economy," at www.quran. org/library/articles/interest.htm.

6. Executive Committee of the Editorial Board, Lewis N. Dembitz, and Joseph Jacobs, "Usury" at www.jewishencyclopedia.com/view.jsp?artid=58&letter=U.

7. Martin Luther, "On Trading and Usury" at www.lutherdansk.dk/Martin%20 Luther%20-%20On%20trading%20and%20usury%201524/.

8. Adam Smith, *An Inquiry into the Nature and Causes of The Wealth of Nations* (New York: The Modern Library, 1937), p. 339.

9. Ibid., pp. 339–40.

10. Karl Marx, *Capital*, vol. III, part V, "Division of Profit into Interest and Profit of Enterprise. Interest-Bearing Capital," chapter 29: "Component Parts of Bank Capital," at www.marxists.org/archive/marx/works/1894-c3/ch29.htm.

11. John Kay, "Taxpayers Will Fund another Run on the Casino," *Financial Times*, September 16, 2008, at www.ft.com/cms/s/0/770e2a94-840d-11dd-bf00- 000077b07658.html.

12. Valerie Hansen and Ana Mata-Fink, "Part II: Records from a Seventh-Century Pawnshop in China," in *The Origin of Value: The Financial Innovations that Created Modern Capital Markets*, William N. Goetzmann and K. Geert Rouwenhorst, editors (New York, Oxford University Press, 2005), p. 58. The authors cite a L.S. Yang, "the author of a classic study about pownshops."

13. This is called Grisham's Law—bad money drives good money out of circulation. The debasement of currency leads to more hording of gold and silver, exacerbating the shortages.

14. Let's say I've given my Dutch East India company shares, worth 1,000 guilders, as collateral to get an 800-guilder loan to purchase another sailing ship. If the price of my shares goes down, the person who loaned me the money will want more shares as collateral. But let's say I can protect myself by buying a futures contract for about 50 guilders. That would give me the option (the right) to sell my shares at a specific future date for 1,000 guilders. My downside is protected. The 50 guilders is an insurance policy for the value of my shares.

15. Robert J. Barro and José F. Ursúa, "Macroeconomic Crises since 1870," Brookings Paper on Economic Activity, May 7, 2008, at http://www.econ.yale .edu/seminars/macro/mac08/Barro-081028.pdf.

16. "A Rosen, with blood-red flares or flames vividly streaked on a white ground, and flakes and flashes of the same color at the petals' edge, Semper Augustus was, by all accounts, an extraordinary flower, and one celebrated at the time for its beauty and rarity." From http://penelope.uchicago.edu/~grout/encyclopae dia_romana/aconite/semperaugustus.html.

17. Edward Chancellor, *Devil Take the Hindmost: A History of Financial Speculation* (New York: Plume Books, 2000), p. 16.

18. Ibid, p. 18.

19. bid, p. 19.

20. "Remarks by Chairman Alan Greenspan," at the Annual Dinner and Francis Boyer Lecture of The American Enterprise Institute for Public Policy Research, Washington, D.C., December 5, 1996. "But how do we know when irrational exuberance has unduly escalated asset values, which then become subject to unexpected and prolonged contractions as they have in Japan over the past decade?" At www.federalreserve.gov/boarddocs/speeches/1996/ 19961205.htm.
    However, there are also powerful economic arguments that describe this process as part and parcel of financial markets—that you don't need herd mentality or irrational exuberance to create a bubble. For example, economists John Maynard Keynes and later Hyman Minsky argued that capital markets were inherently unstable, even if we assume rational behavior on the part of the buyers and sellers in the markets. During the past thirty years many of their ideas were dismissed. But the crash of 2008 has brought renewed attention to their theories. We will return to their theories in the last chapters of this book.

21. Money was provided to the government in return for a fixed payment per year in perpetuity.

22. Chancellor, p. 82.

23. Chancellor, p. 108.

24. Ibid., pp. 109–110.

25. Bob Woodward, *The Agenda: Inside the Clinton White House* (New York: Simon and Schuster Paperbacks, 2005) p. 73.

Chapter 4: Learning and Unlearning the Lessons of the Great Depression

1. Ben Bernanke, *Essays on the Great Depression* (Princeton, NJ: Princeton University Press, 2000), p. vii.

2. Herbert Hoover, *The Memoirs of Herbert Hoover*, vol. 3, *The Great Depression, 1929–1941* (Scranton, PA: The Haddon Craftsmen, Inc., 1952), p. 30.

3. Edward Chancellor, *Devil Take the Hindmost: A History of Financial Speculation* (New York: Plume Books, 2000), p. 197.

4. For an excellent selection of quotations, see Colin J. Seymour, "1927–1933 Chart of Pompous Prognosticators," June 2001, at www.gold-eagle.com/ editorials_01/seymour062001.html.

5. John Maynard Keynes, *The General Theory of Employment, Interest and Money* (New York: Harcourt, Brace and World, 1964), p. 159.

6. In modern "fractional" banking, banks only keep on hand a small fraction of the total deposited with them by consumers and businesses. The rest is put out on loan. Almost all of the time this is sufficient to cover day-to-day withdrawals. However, should large numbers of depositors request their money at the same time (as during economic panics) banks can go bust.

7. Traders can speculate that a currency is over- or undervalued. If the bets are very large and in the same direction, the value of a currency can drastically change, which, in turn, can cause large dislocations and disruptions in the economies relying on that currency.

8. The Bretton Woods agreement permitted countries to exchange dollars for a fixed amount of gold—$35 per ounce. By the 1960s the quantity of dollars circulating in the world greatly exceeded the amount of gold backing it. Should several other countries attempt to exchange their dollars for gold at the same time, the United States would run out of gold, just like a bank facing a run of consumers rushing to get their deposits.

9. Milton Friedman, "The Social Responsibility of Business Is to Increase Its Profits," *New York Times Magazine*, September 13, 1970, reproduced at www.colorado.edu/studentgroups/libertarians/issues/friedman-soc-resp-business.html.

10. "Remarks by Governor Ben S. Bernanke before the New York Chapter of the National Association for Business Economics, New York, New York, October 15, 2002, "Asset-Price 'Bubbles' and Monetary Policy," at www.federalreserve.gov/boarddocs/speeches/2002/20021015/default.htm.

11. U.S. Department of Commerce, Bureau of the Census, *Statistical Abstract of the United States, 1996* (Washington, DC: U.S. GPO, 1996), p. 330; and Edward N. Wolff, *The Rich Get Increasingly Richer* (Washington, DC: Economic Policy Institute, 1992), p. 30.

12. Actually, there is little empirical evidence to support the universality of this idea. Those with home insurance, for example, usually take more care in protecting their property. Nevertheless, most financial analysts are convinced "moral hazards" pose severe risks.

13. Paul Oranika, "Alan Greenspan Adds His Voice to the Hedge Fund Regulation Controversy Again," HedgeCo.net, August 25, 2004, at www.hedgeco.net/news/08/2004/alan-greenspan-adds-his-voice-hedge-fund-regulation-controversy-again.html.

Chapter 5: The Oracle Blesses Derivatives, the Newest Game in the Casino

1. James L. Bothwell, "Financial Derivatives: Actions Needed to Protect the Financial System," Testimony before the Subcommittee on Environment, Credit, and Rural Development, Committee on Agriculture, June 14, 1994 (Washington, DC: United States General Accounting Office), GAO/T-660-94-169, p. 1, available at http://archive.gao.gov/t2pbat3/151816.pdf.

2. Ibid., pp. 1–2.

3. Ibid., p. 2.

4. Ibid.

5. Ibid., p. 3.

6. There's some ambiguity about who has earned the title of "Oracle." We follow along with E. Ray Canterbery's book, *Alan Greenspan: The Oracle behind the Curtain* (Hackensack, NJ: World Scientific Publishing Co., 2006); but some financial insiders also give the title to Warren Buffett.

7. Frank Partnoy, *Infectious Greed: How Deceit and Risk Corrupted the Financial Markets* (New York: Henry Holt and Company, 2003), p. 151.

8. "Statement by Alan Greenspan, Chairman, Board of Governors of the Federal Reserve System, before the Committee on Banking, Housing and Urban Affairs, U.S. Senate, January 5, 1995," *Federal Reserve Bulletin*, March 1995, at http://findarticles.com/p/articles/mi_m4126/is_/ai_16795142.

9. Partnoy, p. 151.

10. For more technical definitions see Gunter Meissner, *Credit Derivatives: Application, Pricing, and Risk Management* (Malden, MA: Blackwell Publishing, 2005).

11. Satyajit Das, *Traders, Guns and Money: Knowns and Unknowns in the Dazzling World of Derivatives* (New York: Prentice Hall/Financial Times, 2006), p. 7.

12. Ibid., p. 214.

13. Ibid.

14. Ibid., p. 127.

15. Ibid., p. 215.
16. Bob Baker, "Psychic, Astrologer Influenced Citron, Grand Jury Told," December 28, 1995, at www.newsthinking.com/story.cfm?SID=130.
17. James Sterngold, "Orange County Bankruptcy: The Poor Feel the Most Pain, *New York Times*, December 5, 1995, at www.nytimes.com/1995/12/05/us/orange-county-bankruptcy-the-poor-feel-the-most-pain.html.
18. According to Investopedia.com, *arbitrage* is "The simultaneous purchase and sale of an asset in order to profit from a difference in the price. It is a trade that profits by exploiting price differences of identical or similar financial instruments, on different markets or in different forms. Arbitrage exists as a result of market inefficiencies; it provides a mechanism to ensure prices do not deviate substantially from fair value for long periods of time."
19. Partnoy, p. 255.
20. Ibid., p. 260.
21. Ibid.
22. For this and the following quotes from Born, see "A Conversation with Brooksley Born," originally published in *Washington Lawyer*, October 2003, available at www.dcbar.org/for_lawyers/resources/legends_in_the_law/born.cfm.
23. Peter S. Goodman, "The Reckoning: Taking Hard New Look at a Greenspan Legacy," *New York Times*, October 8, 2008, at www.nytimes.com/2008/10/09/business/economy/09greenspan.html.
24. David Corn, "Foreclosure Phil," *Mother Jones*, July/August 2008, at www.motherjones.com/news/feature/2008/07/foreclosure-phil.html. But give the guy credit: In this new century, our financial industry *has* led the world . . . right over the cliff.
25. "A Conversation with Brooksley Born."

Chapter 6: Getting the Story Backwards

1. *Morning Joe*, MSNBC, September 17, 2008, at www.youtube.com/watch?v=xl1H1Eg4GJU.
2. "Prepared Testimony of Michael S. Barr, Professor of Law, University of Michigan Law School before the Committee on Financial Services, U.S. House of Representatives Hearing On 'The Community Reinvestment Act: Thirty Years of Accomplishments, But Challenges Remain,'" February 13, 2008, p. 4, at www.house.gov/financialservices/hearing110/barr021308.pdf.
3. Janet L. Yellen, "Opening Remarks to the 2008 National Interagency Community Reinvestment Conference," March 31, 2008, at www.frbsf.org/news/speeches/2008/0331.html.
4. "The Community Reinvestment Act: A Welcome Anomaly in the Foreclosure Crisis. Indications That the CRA Deterred Irresponsible Lending in the 15 Most Populous U.S. Metropolitan Areas," January 7, 2008, prepared by Traiger and Hinckley, LLP, at www.traigerlaw.com/publications/traiger_hinckley_llp_cra_foreclosure_study_1-7-08.pdf.
5. Peter J. Wallison and Charles W. Calomiris, "The Last Trillion Dollar Commitment, the Destruction of Fannie Mae and Freddie Mac," American Enterprise Institute Financial Services Outlook, AEI On-line, at www.aei.org/publications/pubID.28704/pub_detail.asp.
6. Stuart Taylor, "When Fannie and Freddie Opened the Floodgates," *National Review*, October 18, 2008, at www.nationaljournal.com/njmagazine/or_20081018_3384.php.

7. "Is Capitalism Dead? The Market That Failed Was Not Exactly Free," *Washington Post* editorial, October 20, 2008, p. A14, at www.washingtonpost. com/wp-dyn/content/article/2008/10/19/AR2008101901416.html.

8. Wallison and Calomiris.

9. Dean Baker, *Plunder and Blunder: The Rise and Fall of the Bubble Economy* (Sausalito, CA: PoliPointPress, 2009), p. 85.

10. *New York Times*, "An Estimate: Adding Up Bank Losses," a chart based on RGE Monitor data, February 12, 2009, at www.nytimes.com/imagepages/2009/02/12/business/20090213_INSOLVENT_graphic.html.

11. Peter S. Goodman, "Taking Hard New Look at a Greenspan Legacy," *New York Times*, October 8, 2008, at www.nytimes.com/2008/10/09/business/economy/09greenspan.html.

12. For a concise description of the New Deal housing programs, see Robert J. Shiller, *The Subprime Solution* (Princeton, NJ: Princeton University Press, 2008), pp. 11–16.

13. For a description of Ginny Mae see www.ginniemae.gov/about/about. asp?subTitle=About.

14. Richard Tomlinson and David Evans, "The Ratings Charade," *Bloomberg Markets Magazine*, July 2007, at www.bloomberg.com/news/marketsmag/ratings.html.

15. For an entertaining introduction, see the video, "Crisis Explainer: Uncorking CDOs," by *Marketplace* senior editor Paddy Hirsch at http://vimeo.com/1876936. Also, Portfolio.com provides an animated flow chart, "What's a C.D.O.?" at www.portfolio.com/interactive-features/2007/12/cdo.

16. Adapted from Paddy Hirsch's video noted above.

17. CDOs can also be constructed from pools of credit card payments, student loan payments, car leases, or any other cash flow—the riskier the better.

18. For more complex versions, see an excellent set of videos by David Harper posted on You Tube including "Synthetic CDO that Fails in Subprime Securitization," at www.youtube.com/watch?v=-8vmzvfEuk0.

19. David Evans, "Banks Sell 'Toxic Waste' CDOs to Calpers, Texas Teachers Fund," Bloomberg, June 1, 2008, at www.bloomberg.com/apps/news?pid=newsarchive&sid=aQWoYszGR6w0. Many pension funds have rules that allow them to buy some lower-rated (but not junk) securities, so that these are, at most, a small percentage of the total pension holdings. Derivative dealers found ways to package the toxic waste with government bonds so that it would seem that the investment was protected, and so could get these equity tranches rated above junk status. More recently, the ratings have been lowered to junk and so those investments are now off-limits to pension funds.

20. David Evans, "The Poison in Your Pension," Bloomberg Markets, July 2007, at www.bloomberg.com/news/marketsmag/pension.html.

21. For a succinct description of this conveyor belt, see Charles R. Morris, *The Trillion Dollar Meltdown: Easy Money, High Rollers, and the Great Credit Crash* (New York: Public Affairs, 2008), pp. 68–72.

Chapter 7: Financial Weapons of Mass Destruction

1. For an excellent description of Demchak's efforts, see Jesse Eisinger, "The $58 Trillion Elephant in the Room," Porfolio.com, October 15, 2008, at www.portfolio.com/views/columns/wall-street/2008/10/15/Credit-Derivatives-Role-in-Crash#page5.

2. "An Estimate: Adding up Bank Losses," a chart based on RGE Monitor data, *New York Times*, February 12, 2009, at www.nytimes.com/image pages/2009/02/12/business/20090213_INSOLVENT_graphic.html.

3. Thomas Tan, "Why Wall Street Needs Credit Default Swaps," at http://news .goldseek.com/GoldSeek/1208412360.php.

4. "Prepackaged Bankruptcy Could Trigger GM CDS: Analyst," Reuters, December 5, 2008, at www.reuters.com/article/asiaDealsNews/ idUSTRE4B44NR20081205.

5. "Testimony of Robert Pickel, Chief Executive Officer, International Swaps and Derivatives Association before the Senate Committee on Agriculture," October 15, 2008, p. 4, at http://agriculture.house.gov/testimony/110/h81015/Pickel.pdf.

6. The following examples are adapted from a primer on credit default swaps that first appeared on the web on May 2, 2008. I'm working from the version posted by Daniel Amerman, "AIG's Dangerous Collapse & A Credit Derivatives Risk Primer," September 17, 2008, at www.financialsense.com/fsu/editorials/amer-man/2008/0917.html.

7. That would be a 2.4 percent fee or what they call in the trade 240 basis points—a basis point being 0.01 percent.

8. Amerman.

9. Jane Baird, "UPDATE 2-CDS Payout for 3 Icelandic Banks About $7.3 Bln," Reuters, November 6, 2008, at www.reuters.com/article/rbssBanks/ idUSL628743320081106.

10. The value could be 99 cents on the dollar, which Fanny and Freddie bonds fetched. Or it could be more like Lehman Brothers bonds, which fetched only 8 cents on the dollar.

11. Louise Story and Eric Dash, "Banks are Likely to Hold Tight to Bailout Money," *New York Times*, October 16, 2008, at www.nytimes.com/2008/10/17/ business/17bank.html.

Chapter 8: Fantasy Finance Meets Reality: The Great Crash of 2008

1. Robert J. Shiller, *The Subprime Solution* (Princeton, NJ: Princeton University Press, 2008), pp. 32–33.

2. Danielle DiMartino and John V. Duca, "The Rise and Fall of Subprime Mortgages," *Economic Letter—Insights from the Federal Reserve Bank of Dallas* 2, no. 11 (November 2007), Federal Reserve Bank of Dallas at http://dallasfed.org/ research/eclett/2007/el0711.html.

3. "S&P/Case-Shiller Home Price Factsheet," p. 1, downloaded March 22, 2009, from www2.standardandpoors.com/portal/site/sp/en/us/page.arti-cle/0,0,0,0,1145771405992.html.

4. Nell Henderson, "Bernanke: There's No Housing Bubble to Go Bust," *Washington Post*, October 27, 2005, at www.washingtonpost.com/wp-dyn/ content/article/2005/10/26/AR2005102602255.html. One must also wonder what kind of rose-colored glasses Bernanke had on when he looked at the fundamentals. For example, as we see in chart 2 on page 14, "Actual Wages vs. Productivity-Enhanced Wages," real wages for most Americans were as stagnant in 2005 as they'd been for the prior thirty-plus years.

5. I got hooked on the game through my roommates, sports writers Larry Fine (who owned a fantasy team) and Ouisie Shapiro (who was the league's first "commissioner"). In those days Ouisie had to do the statistics each week by

hand, and I did what I could to help. Soon, Larry brought me in to become his partner in what has become the fabled fantasy franchise, the Fine Tooners. For several years I wrote the statistical sections of *How to Win at Rotisserie Baseball* by Peter Golenbach. Larry and I still manage the Fine Tooners.

6. Frank Partnoy and David A. Skeel Jr., "The Promise and Perils of Credit Derivatives," University of Pennsylvania Law School, Scholarship at Penn Law paper 125, September 11, 2006, p. 35, at http://lsr.nellco.org/upenn/wps/papers/125.

7. Mark Landler, "US Credit Crisis Adds Gloom in Norway," *New York Times*, December 2, 2007, at www.nytimes.com/2007/12/02/world/europe/02norway.html.

8. Jay Shaylor, Lauren Pearle, and Tina Babarovic, "AIG's Small London Office May Have Lost $500B," ABC News, March 10, 2009, at http://abcnews.go.com/print?id=7045889.

9. Edmund L. Andrews and Peter Baker, "AIG Planning Huge Bonuses after $170 Billion Bailout," *New York Times*, March 14, 2009, at www.nytimes.com/2009/03/15/business/15AIG.html.

10. Frank Partnoy, *Infectious Greed: How Deceit and Risk Corrupted the Financial Markets* (New York: Henry Holt and Company, 2003), p. 383.

11. Ben Bernanke, C-SPAN video archive of testimony before the House Financial Services Committee, February 25, 2009, video time code 01:43:30, at www.c-spanarchives.org/library/indexphp?main_page=product_video_info&products_id=284296-3&showVid=true.

Chapter 9: The End of Fantasy Finance?

1. Eric Lipton and Stephen Labaton, "Deregulator Looks Back, Unswayed," *New York Times*, November 17, 2008, at www.nytimes.com/2008/11/17/business/economy/17gramm.html.

2. Thomas L. Friedman, "If Larry and Sergey Asked for a Loan . . .," New York Times, October 26, 2008, at www.nytimes.com/2008/10/26/opinion/26friedman.html.

3. Ibid.

4. Frank Partnoy, *Infectious Greed: How Deceit and Risk Corrupted the Financial Markets* (New York: Henry Holt and Company, 2003), p. 385.

5. For the record, although my sample is very small, some of the brightest people I've met work for rating agencies.

6. Partnoy, pp. 387–88.

7. Ibid., p. 388.

8. Ibid.

9. Thomas Philippon and Ariell Reshef, "Wages and Human Capital in the U.S. Financial Industry: 1909–2006," NBER Working Paper no. 14644, January 2009, p. 32, at http://pages.stern.nyu.edu/~tphilipp/papers/pr_rev15.pdf.

10. From Chairman Henry Waxman's opening statement, October 22, 2008, House Committee on Oversight and Government Reform, "Credit Rating Agencies and the Financial Crisis."

11. Shannon Moody to Rahul Dilip Shah, April 5, 2007, at http://oversight.house.gov/documents/20081022112325.pdf.

12. Richard Tomlinson and David Evans, "The Ratings Charade," Bloomberg Markets, July 2007, at www.bloomberg.com/news/marketsmag/ratings.html.

13. Ibid.
14. "Testimony of Dr. Alan Greenspan," House Committee of Government Oversight and Reform, October 23, 2008, p. 3, at http://oversight.house.gov/documents/20081023100438.pdf.
15. Partnoy, p. 406.
16. Ibid., p. 403. In fairness, Partnoy may no longer view derivatives in such a positive light, as evidenced by his 2006 paper with Skeel cited in chapter 8.
17. Ibid., p. 390.
18. "Testimony of Dr. Alan Greenspan," p. 2.
19. As of November 2008 the Bush administration backed away from the original TARP plan to buy toxic-waste assets from financial companies in favor of direct cash infusions. They said the process would take too long. But in February 2008, the Obama administration returned to the plan of buying up the toxic assets through a public-private partnership that would protect investors from losses. That plan was launched in late March 2009 and brought great cheers from Wall Street.
20. This example assumes the bank was subject to an 8 percent reserve requirement, which is about where it generally is in practice. If the banks receive a $100 dollar deposit, then they can lend out $92. When that $92 gets deposited into a bank, then $84.64 can be lent out, and so on. The total loaned out will add up to $1,150.
21. Charles R. Morris, *Trillion Dollar Meltdown: Easy Money, High Rollers, and the Great Credit Crash* (New York: Public Affairs, 2008), p. xii.
22. See George Soros's testimony before the House Committee on Oversight and Government Reform, November 13, 2008, at www.c-spanarchives.org/library/index.php?main_page=product_video_info&products_id=282391-2. Soros makes clear he believes the problem is inherent to normal-functioning financial markets, and that it stems from the uncontrolled increase in leverage.

Chapter 10: Proposals Wall Street Won't Like

1. Iris J. Lav and Elizabeth McNichol, "State Budget Troubles Worsen," Center on Budget and Policy Priorities, updated March 13, 2009, at www.cbpp.org/cms/?fa=view&id=711.
2. Adam Nossiter, "Alabama School Districts Feel the Economic Pinch as Tax Revenues Decline," *New York Times*, November 4, 2008, at www.nytimes.com/2008/11/05/us/05alabama.html.
3. David Brooks, "A Date with Scarcity," *New York Times*, November 3, 2008, at www.nytimes.com/2008/11/04/opinion/04brooks.html.
4. Niall Ferguson, *The Ascent of Money: A Financial History of the World* (New York: Penguin, 2008), pp. 4–5.
5. Dean Baker, in *Plunder and Blunder: The Rise and Fall of the Bubble Economy* (Sausalito, CA: PoliPointPress, 2009), p. 131, estimates that a "tax on the purchase or sale of an option of credit default swap might be 0.01 percent of the price . . . [and] can easily raise $150 billion a year."
6. Daniel B. Klein, "Economists Against the FDA," The Independent Institute, September 1, 2000, citing Durk Pearson and Sandy Shaw, *Freedom of Informed Choice: FDA Versus Nutrient Supplements* (Neptune, NJ: Common Sense Press, 1993), p. 39, at www.independent.org/publications/article.asp?id=279.
7. Adam Davidson, "Wisconsin School Investment Has Worldwide Implications,"

Weekend Edition Sunday, November 2, 2008, at www.npr.org/templates/story/story.php?storyId=96414824.

8. Variable rate municipal bonds are the municipal equivalent of adjustable mortgages—the rate the public agency must pay varies, in some cases, daily. During low interest-rate periods, public agencies can save money. But the rates can rise rapidly. Also these bonds depended on insurance provided by companies that lost billions on insuring CDOs and other toxic debt. When the insurers were downgraded, the rates on the variable rate municipal bonds shot up, costing public agencies billions of dollars. See Anastasija Johnson, "Bond Insurer Troubles Hit Variable-Rate Munis," Reuters, January 24, 2008, at www.reuters.com/article/companyNews/idUSN2423063820080124.

9. This is a particularly strong formulation of the problem. However, it is extremely difficult to find any evidence that suggests that, on the whole, these financial instruments contribute to the public good. Hopefully, more careful academics will develop an objective way to assess them.

10. "Statement of George Soros before the U.S. House of Representatives Committee on Oversight and Government Reform," November 13, 2008, p. 10, at http://oversight.house.gov/documents/20081113120114.pdf.

Chapter 11: Proposals Wall Street *Really* Won't Like

1. "The Forbes 400," *Forbes*, October issues, 1982–2008.

2. These billionaires didn't make all of their money in the financial sector. Bill Gates, Michael Bloomberg, and others gained their riches through stock appreciation of the firms they started. But many of the top 400 have strong ties to the financial sector. Also, there's a nontrivial connection to the rise of stock equities and financial booms.

3. Louise Story, "Top Hedge Fund Managers Do Well in a Down Year," *New York Times*, March 24, 2009, at www.nytimes.com/2009/03/25/business/25hedge.html.

4. "President Obama's Remarks on Executive Pay," *New York Times*, February 4, 2009, at www.nytimes.com/2009/02/04/us/politics/04text-obama.html.

5. "TARP Recipients Paid Out $114 Million for Politicking Last Year," Center for Responsive Politics, press release, February 4, 2009, at www.opensecrets.org/news/2009/02/tarp-recipients-paid-out-114-m.html.

6. Robert Siegel, "At Auto Show, GM Seeks to Shift Perceptions," *All Things Considered*, January 12, 2009, at www.npr.org/templates/story/story.php?storyId=99253055.

7. Niall Ferguson, *The Ascent of Money: A Financial History of the World* (New York: Penguin, 2008), p. 5.

8. Robert H. Frank and Philip J. Cook, *The Winner-Take-All Society* (New York: Penguin, 1995), p. 90.

9. Ibid., p. 94.

10. Thomas Philippon and Ariell Reshef, "Wages and Human Capital in the U.S. Financial Industry: 1909–2006," NBER Working Paper no. 14644, January 2009, NBER Program, p. 30, at http://pages.stern.nyu.edu/~tphilipp/papers/pr_rev15.pdf.

11. Paul Krugman, "Policy, Politics, and Equality," transcript of an address to the Economic Policy Institute, February 22, 2007, at www.epi.org/publications/entry/webfeatures_viewpoints_politics_policy_inequality.

12. Robert Reich, "Why Financial CEOs Earn So Much More Than Real-Economy CEOs," *Marketplace*, October 31, 2007, at www.robertreich.org/reich/20071031 .asp.

13. "President Obama's Remarks on Executive Pay."

14. James F. Reda quoted in Edmund L. Andrews and Eric Dash, "Stimulus Plan Puts New Limits on Executive Pay," *New York Times*, February 13, 2009, at www.nytimes.com/2009/02/14/business/economy/14pay.html.

15. Alan Johnson, quoted in ibid.

16. Andrew Ross Sorkin, "A Bridge Loan? U.S. Should Guide G.M. in a Chapter 11," *New York Times*, November 17, 2008, at www.nytimes.com/2008/11/18/ business/economy/18sorkin.html.

17. See Sam Pizzigati and Howard Saunders (illustrator), *The Maximum Wage: A Common-Sense Prescription for Revitalizing America By Taxing the Very Rich* (New York: The Apex Press, 1992). Also see his website at http://toomuchonline.org.

18. Robert H. Frank, "Should Congress Put a Cap on Executive Pay?" *New York Times*, January 3, 2009, at www.nytimes.com/2009/01/04/business/ economy/04view.html.

19. Jamal A. Rashed and Subarna K. Samanta, "The Productivity-Wage Gap and the Recent Stock Price Increase: An Analysis," *International Review of Economics & Finance* 14, no. 2 (2005), pp. 171 and 179.

20. For an informative and entertaining explanation of the systemic collapse that builds from the productivity/wage gap, see economist Rick Wolff's lecture at www.vimeo.com/1962208.

21. For a detailed description of EFCA, see the AFL-CIO website at www.aflcio .org/joinaunion/voiceatwork/efca/whatis.cfm.

22. Kate Bronfenbrenner, "Uneasy Terrain: The Impact of Capital Mobility on Workers, Wages, and Union Organizing," Cornell University ILR School Research Studies and Reports (September 2000), p. 43, at http://digital commons.ilr.cornell.edu/reports/3/.

23. John Schmitt and Ben Zipperer, "Dropping the Ax: Illegal Firings during Union Election Campaigns, 1951–2007," Center for Economic and Policy Research, March 2009, Summary, at www.cepr.net/documents/publications/dropping-the- ax-2009-03.pdf.

24. Patrice Woeppel, "On Worker Deaths," Center for Popular Economics, March 17, 2009, at www.fguide.org/?p=228.

25. In fact, Kate Bronfenbrenner's survey (p. 44) found that 20 percent of all employers reacted to a union campaign by increasing wages, even before the unionization effort succeeded.

26. See David Card and Alan Krueger's 1997 book, *Myth and Measurement: The New Economics of the Minimum Wage* (Princeton, NJ: Princeton University Press), which provides real-world evidence that the minimum wage does not kill jobs. Also see Robert Pollin and Stephanie Luce, *The Living Wage: Building a Fair Economy* (New York: The New Press, 2000), and the research published at the Political Economy Research Institute, Labor Markets and Living Wage Program at www.peri.umass.edu/Labor-Market-L.197.0.html.

27. Mike McIntire, "Bailout Is a Windfall to Banks, if Not to Borrowers," *New York Times*, January 17, 2009, p. 1, at www.nytimes.com/2009/01/18/ business/18bank.html.

28. "House of Cards," CNBC documentary, aired on February 12, 2009. Quotation found at http://forums.hornfans.com/php/wwwthreads/showflat.php?Cat=&Board=westmall&Number=5888128&page=0&view=collapsed&sb=5&o=0&fpart=.
29. Bob Dylan, "Stuck Inside of Mobile With the Memphis Blues Again," at www.bobdylan.com/#/songs/stuck-inside-mobile-memphis-blues-again.

Glossary
1. www.investopedia.com/terms/a/arbitrage.asp.
2. www.wikinvest.com/wiki/Collateralized_debt_obligation_(CDO).
3. http://en.wikipedia.org/wiki/Securities.
4. www.investopedia.com/terms/h/hedgefund.asp.
5. Zachary A. Goldfard and David Cho, "Hedge Funds Making Way for Government Regulation," *Washington Post*, March 14, 2009, at www.washingtonpost.com/wp-dyn/content/article/2009/03/13/AR2009031303063.html.

Index

Les Leopold cofounded and directs two nonprofit educational organizations, the Labor Institute and the Public Health Institute, where he designs research and educational programs on occupational safety and health, the environment, and economics. He helped form the Blue-Green Alliance, which brings together major labor unions, such as the United Steelworkers and Service Employees International Union, and environmental groups, such as the Sierra Club and Natural Resources Defense Council, to promote the growth of America's green economy. Leopold is author of the award-winning biography *The Man Who Hated Work and Loved Labor: The Life and Times of Tony Mazzocchi*. He lives with his family in Montclair, New Jersey. Leopold attended Oberlin College and holds a masters in public administration from Princeton University's Woodrow Wilson School of Public and International Affairs.